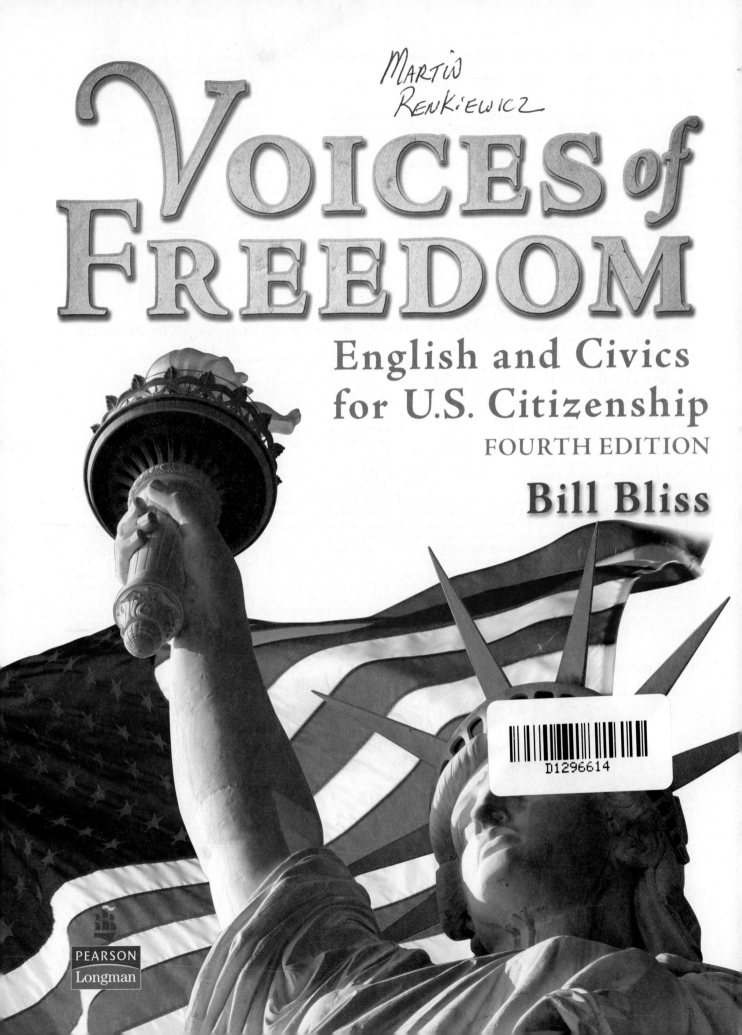

Martin
Renkiewicz

Voices of Freedom

English and Civics
for U.S. Citizenship

FOURTH EDITION

Bill Bliss

PEARSON
Longman

Voices of Freedom: English and Civics for U.S. Citizenship, Fourth Edition

Pearson Education, 10 Bank Street, White Plains, NY 10606

Dedicated to Benjamin and Flora Bliss, Nathan and Sophia Bliss, and Nat and Betty Meister.

The cooperation of U.S. Citizenship and Immigration Services, Washington District Office, Fairfax, Virginia, is gratefully acknowledged.

Editorial director: Pam Fishman
Vice president, director of design and production: Rhea Banker
Director of electronic production: Aliza Greenblatt
Manager of electronic production services: Warren Fischbach
Director of manufacturing: Patrice Fraccio
Senior manufacturing buyer: Dave Dickey
Prepress buyer: Ray Keating

Marketing director: Oliva Fernandez
Production editor: Diane Cipollone
Assistant editor: Katherine Keyes
Development editor/Photo coordinator: Mary Perrotta Rich
Senior digital layout specialist: Wendy Wolf
Text and cover design: Wendy Wolf

Photo Credits
Cover Shutterstock and Getty Images, Inc./Purestock.
Back cover *left and right* Paul I. Tañedo.

Page **1**, **2**, **3**, **4**, **6**, **8**, **10**, **14**, **16**, **18**, **20**, **21**, **34**, **53** (*top*), **71**, **87**, **104**, **121**, **161**, **181**, **208**, **213**, **214**, **215**, **216**, **217**, **218**, **219**, **220**, **226**, **227**, and **241** by Paul I. Tañedo.

Page **iv**: © Jim Young/Reuters/Corbis; **25** Getty Images Inc. - Stone Allstock; **26**: Mapresources.com; **30** *top left*: Ed Oakes/iStockphoto.com, *top right*: Courtesy of www.iStockphoto.com, *bottom left*: Stephen Finn/iStockphoto.com, *bottom right*: iStockphoto.com; **31** *top left*: Sam Valtenbergs/iStockphoto.com, *top right*: William Blacke/iStockphoto.com, *middle left*: Brandon Seidel/Shutterstock, *middle right*: Lubomir Jendrol/iStockphoto.com, *bottom left*: Jeremy Edwards/iStockphoto.com, *bottom right*: David M. Albrecht/Shutterstock; **32** *top*: Mapresources.com, *bottom*: Mapresources.com; **35**: Justin Williford/Shutterstock; **39** *left*: © Craig Tuttle/Corbis, *top right*: Sarah Nicholl/Shutterstock, *bottom right*: Boston Globe/Getty Images; **40**: Joe Gough/Shutterstock; **42** *left*: AP/Wide World Photos, *top right*: AP Images/NASA, *bottom right*: Thomas E. Franklin/Getty Images; **43** *top* and *middle*: Sarah Nicholl/Shutterstock, *bottom*: Boston Globe/Getty Images; **47** *top*, *left to right*: Dieter Spears/iStockphoto.com, Joseph C. Justice Jr./iStockphoto.com, John Kuo/iStockphoto.com, *bottom*, *left to right*: Chip Somodevilla/Getty images, Patrick Fallon/ZUMA Press, Inc/Alamy Stock Photo, AP Images/Pablo Martinez Monsivais; **48** *left to right*: Jeremy Edwards/iStockphoto.com, Joseph C. Justice Jr./iStockphoto.com, John Kuo/iStockphoto.com; **50** *top*: iStockphoto.com, *middle*: iStockphoto.com *bottom*: iStockphoto.com; **53** *bottom*, *left to right*: Dieter Spears/iStockphoto.com, Joseph C. Justice Jr./iStockphoto.com, John Kuo/iStockphoto.com; **57** *top*, *left to right*: U.S. Senate photo, U.S. government website, © Brooks Kraft/Corbis, Representative Hinojosa website, *bottom left*: Patrick Fallon/ZUMA Press, Inc/Alamy Stock Photo, *bottom right*: AP Images/Pablo Martinez Monsivais; **58**: U.S. Senate photo; **60** *top*: Xinhva/Alamy Stock Photo, *bottom*: dpa picture alliance/Alamy Stock Photo; **62** *top*: Richard Ellis/Alamy Stock Photo, *bottom*: Chip Somodevilla/Consolidated News Photos/dpa picture alliance/Alamy Stock Photo; **63** *top*: Nojustice/E+/Getty Images, *bottom*: Richard Ellis/Alamy Stock Photo; **65** *bottom*: U.S. Department of Commerce; **66** *top*, *left to right*: U.S. Department of Agriculture, Shutterstock, U.S. Department of Commerce, Tim Boyle/Getty Images, *row 2*, *left to right*: U.S. Department of Defense Visual Information Center, © Kim Komenich/San Francisco Chronicle/Corbis, U.S. Department of Education, © luminaimages/Shutterstock, *row 3*, *left to right*: U.S. Department of Energy, Manfred Steinbach/iStockphoto.com, U.S. Department of Health and Human Services, Spencer Platt/Getty Images, *row 4*, *left to right*: U.S. Department of Homeland Security, John Moore/Getty Images, U.S. Department of Housing and Urban Development, Kim Steele/Alamy, *bottom*, *left to right*: U.S. Department of the Interior, James M. Phelps, Jr./Shutterstock, U.S. Department of Labor, Scott Olson/Getty Images; **67** *top*, *left to right*: U.S. State Department, Tomohiro Ohsumi/Getty Images, U.S. Department of Transportation, © Mark Peterson/Corbis,

(continued on p. x)

Library of Congress Cataloging-in-Publication Data

Bliss, Bill.
    Voices of freedom : English and civics for U.S. citizenship/Bill Bliss.—4th ed.
        p. cm.
    Includes index.
    ISBN 978-0-13-236628-1 (sb w/audio cd -- ISBN 978-0-13-813159-3 (teacher's guide)
        1. United States -- Politics and government. 2. United States -- History.
    I. Title.

JK1758.B585 2010   2009013789
320.473—dc21

ISBN 0-13-236628-2
ISBN 978-0-13-236628-1

Pearson Longman on the Web
PearsonLongman.com offers online resources for teachers and students. Access our Companion Websites, our online catalog, and our local offices around the world.

Visit us at pearsonlongman.com.

Printed in the United States of America

CONTENTS

Scope and Sequence

Unit	Topics	Grammar	Functional Expressions	USCIS Civics Test Questions	USCIS Reading Vocabulary	USCIS Writing Vocabulary	EL/Civics Enrichment
A	• Personal information • Identification cards • Alphabet • Numbers	• To be • WH-questions	• Clarifying		N-400 Application for Naturalization form	N-400 Application for Naturalization form	• Civic participation: Forms of personal identification • Project: Making a list of emergency telephone numbers • Community Issues: Discussing difficulties using emergency services in the community
B	• Personal information • Months of the year • Dates • Family members	• To be • WH-questions • Yes/No questions • Short answers	• Asking for repetition • Clarifying • Expressing lack of understanding • Verifying information		N-400 Application for Naturalization form	N-400 Application for Naturalization form	• Civic participation: Meeting people in the school • Bulletin board project: Writing a paragraph about oneself and making a bulletin board display • Calendar project: Making a class calendar
1	• Maps & geography • States & capitals • Famous U.S. landmarks • U.S. territories • *America the Beautiful*	• To be • WH-questions • Yes/No questions • Short answers	• Asking for repetition • Clarifying	88, 89, 90, 91, 92, 93, 94, 95	capital city country has is largest most north of people south the United States what	Alaska Canada capital has is largest Mexico most New York City north of people south the United States Washington, D.C.	• Civic participation: Using a local street map • Project: Making a tourist map for visitors to the community • Internet activity: Visiting U.S. states & territories online

CORRELATION and PLACEMENT KEY

Voices of Freedom correlates with the following standards-based curriculum levels and assessment system score ranges:

NRS (National Reporting System) Educational Functioning Level	Low & High Beginning Low Intermediate
CASAS (Comprehensive Adult Student Assessment System) Reading/Listening	181–210
CASAS Writing	136–225
BEST Plus (Basic English Skills Test)	401–472
BEST Oral Interview	16–50
BEST Literacy	21–67
TABE CLASE-E Total Reading & Writing	395–514
TABE CLASE-E Total Listening & Speaking	408–525

Unit	Topics	Grammar	Functional Expressions	USCIS Civics Test Questions	USCIS Reading Vocabulary	USCIS Writing Vocabulary	EL/Civics Enrichment
2	• The flag of the United States • The Pledge of Allegiance	• There is/There are • Singular/plural • Has/has • WH-questions	• Apologizing • Asking for repetition	52, 96, 97	American flag are colors country does have/has how many in is largest most on people state the United States Washington, D.C. what	Alaska and blue California capital fifty (50) flag has is largest most of people red state the United States Washington, D.C. white	• Civic participation: Discussion about the U.S. flag • Bulletin board project: Flags of the world • Internet activity: Searching for information about the flag
3	• Branches of government: legislative, executive, judicial • Checks & balances / Separation of powers	• Simple present tense • Has/has • Can • To be	• Apologizing • Asking for repetition	13, 14, 15	Congress do does in is lives meet of President Senators the United States where White House who	Congress in is lives meet/meets of President Senators the United States Washington, D.C. White House	• Civic participation: Preparing for a field trip to visit the local office of a Congressional representative • Community issues: Brainstorming problems, issues, and opinions to share with a Congressional representative • Internet activity: Visiting a representative's website
4	• The Senate • The House of Representatives • The President & the Vice President • The President's Cabinet • The Supreme Court	• Simple present tense vs. To be • There are • Time expressions • Question formation	• Asking for repetition • Clarifying	16, 17, 18, 19, 20, 21, 22, 23, 24, 25, 26, 27, 28, 29, 30, 31, 32, 33, 34, 35, 36, 37, 38, 39, 40, 47	can citizens Congress do/does elects for government have how many in of people President Senators the United States United States Senators vote when who	can citizens Congress elect fifty (50) for has in November of one hundred (100) people President Senators states the United States	• Civic participation: Visiting the local office of a Congressional representative • Internet activity: Online field trip to the U.S. Capitol • Internet activity: Visiting the White House online

Unit	Topics	Grammar	Functional Expressions	USCIS Civics Test Questions	USCIS Reading Vocabulary	USCIS Writing Vocabulary	EL/Civics Enrichment
5	• Type of government & economic system • The rule of law • Federal & state government • Public officials • The Constitution • The Bill of Rights • The Preamble to the Constitution (We the People)	REVIEW: • Simple present tense • To be • Have/has • Can • Must • WH-Questions	• Clarifying • Indicating understanding	1, 2, 3, 4, 5, 6, 7, 10, 11, 12, 41, 42, 43, 44	Bill of Rights Congress do/does elects for in is live of one people President right the United States vote/votes what when where who	citizens Congress elect for freedom of speech have in lives November of people President the United States vote we White House	• Civic participation: Field trip to local city hall or town government office • Project: Class "Election Day" • Internet activity: Visiting a state's official government website
6	• Native Americans • Christopher Columbus • Discovery • Colonization • Thanksgiving • America (My Country 'Tis of Thee)	• Past tense: Regular verbs • Past tense: Irregular verbs	• Ways to ask questions	58, 59, 87	America Columbus Day come do first in is lived people Thanksgiving the to was when who why	American Indians be Columbus Day first free here in is lived November October people Thanksgiving the to want was	• Civic participation: Field trip to a local supermarket • Project: Celebrating Thanksgiving in the classroom • Internet activity: Visiting Plimoth Plantation online
7	• The Revolutionary War • The Declaration of Independence • Thomas Jefferson • Independence Day (The Fourth of July)	• Past tense: Regular verbs • Past tense: Irregular verbs • Did/didn't	• Saying you don't know	8, 9, 61, 62, 63, 99	capital do first George Washington have in Independence Day is of people President right the United States was what when who	be capital first free have Independence Day in is July of people President right the to United States was Washington Washington, D.C.	• Civic participation: Discussing local government taxes and the services they pay for • Bulletin board project: Time line of historical events in the U.S. & in students' native countries

Unit	Topics	Grammar	Functional Expressions	USCIS Civics Test Questions	USCIS Reading Vocabulary	USCIS Writing Vocabulary	EL/Civics Enrichment
8	• The Constitution • The 13 original states • The *Federalist Papers* • Benjamin Franklin • Branches of government • The Bill of Rights • George Washington	• Past tense: Regular & irregular verbs • Past tense: Was/were • Present tense review	• Hesitating	1, 2, 4, 5, 6, 7, 64, 65, 66, 67, 68, 69, 70	capital city dollar bill Father of Our Country first George Washington in is of on state the United States was what who why	capital Delaware dollar bill Father of Our Country first is New York City of on President state the United States was Washington	• Civic participation: Discussion of how people exercise their rights guaranteed by the First Amendment • Bulletin board project: Newspaper headlines & photographs that are examples of First Amendment rights • Community issues: Discussion of limits on First Amendment rights
9	• The War of 1812 • The *Star-Spangled Banner* (The national anthem) • Expansion • Wars in the 1800s • The Civil War • Abraham Lincoln • Lincoln's Gettysburg Address • Amendments to the Constitution	• Past tense • Ordinal numbers	• Asking for repetition • Clarifying • Indicating understanding	4, 5, 6, 7, 48, 54, 60, 71, 72, 73, 74, 75, 76, 77, 98	Abraham Lincoln Bill of Rights can for in is largest one President Presidents' Day right state the United States vote was what when who	Abraham Lincoln Alaska can citizens Civil War during February for freedom of speech have in is largest of one people President Presidents' Day right state the United States vote was	• Civic participation: Finding amendments in a copy of the Constitution & proposing a new amendment • Debate activity: Debating the voting age in the U.S. • Internet activity: Visiting National Park Service websites
10	• Industrial revolution • Labor movement • Immigration • 20th-century history: World War I The Depression Franklin Delano Roosevelt World War II The United Nations The Cold War, the Korean War, & the Vietnam War The Persian Gulf War • Civil rights movement • Martin Luther King, Jr. • September 11, 2001	• Past tense	• Clarifying • Indicating understanding • Hesitating	78, 79, 80, 81, 82, 83, 84, 85, 86	can citizens come do for have in is Labor Day name of one people right the to United States vote what when who why	and be can citizens come for free freedom of speech have in is Labor Day of people President Senators September the to United States vote	• Internet activity: Online information about famous inventors • Internet activity: Visiting Ellis Island online • Debate activity: Debating whether discrimination exists in the U.S. today

Unit	Topics	Grammar	Functional Expressions	USCIS Civics Test Questions	USCIS Reading Vocabulary	USCIS Writing Vocabulary	EL/Civics Enrichment
11	• National holidays • U.S. Presidents	• Present tense: Review • Past tense		28, 29, 45, 46, 62, 67, 69, 70, 71, 75, 76, 79, 80, 82, 86, 99, 100	Presidents' Day Memorial Day Flag Day Independence Day Labor Day Columbus Day Thanksgiving February May June July September October November in is when	Presidents' Day Memorial Day Flag Day Independence Day Labor Day Columbus Day Thanksgiving February May June July September October November in is	• Civic participation: Discussing U.S. national holidays & how they are celebrated • Internet activity: Learning about Presidents & the White House through the White House website • Project: Writing a short biography of a U.S. President
12	• Citizens' rights • Citizens' responsibilities • Participating in our democracy • The Oath of Allegiance	• Can • Should • Must • Will	• Clarifying • Asking for repetition • Hesitating	1, 2, 3, 4, 5, 6, 7, 8, 9, 10, 11, 12, 45, 49, 50, 51, 53, 54, 55, 56, 57	can citizens do elects for government have in is of one pay people President right the to United States vote what who	and can citizens Congress elect for have in of pay people President right taxes the to United States vote	• Civic participation: Discussing Election Day & visiting a polling place • Community issues: Discussion about rights & responsibilities of all people in their communities & in the nation • Debate activity: Debating whether non-citizens should have the right to vote in local elections

Photo Credits (continued)

middle, left to right: U.S. Department of the Treasury, Alex Wong/Getty Images, Department of Veterans Affairs, © Chris Aschenbrener/Alamy, *bottom, left to right*: U.S. Department of Justice, Scott Olson/Getty Images, The White House Photo Office, Pictorial Press Ltd/Alamy Stock Photo; **68** *top*: AP Images/Pablo Martinez Monsivais, *bottom*: © Brooks Kraft/Corbis; **72** Courtesy of the Office of Rep. Loretta Sanchez; **77** *top, left to right*: Roberto Schmidt/Getty Images, Xinhva/Alamy Stock Photo, Gary Hershorn/Xinhua/Alamy Stock Photo, *bottom, left to right*: Stock Connection Blue/Alamy Stock Photo, Phil Coale/AP Wide World Photos, Justin Sullivan/Getty Images; **78** *top*: Roberto Schmidt/Getty Image, *bottom*: © Mike Segar/Reuters/Corbis; **80** *top, left to right*: Alex Wong/Getty Images, © Jean Louis Atland/Sygma/Corbis, David Furst/Getty Images, Jim Watson/Getty Images, *middle, left to right*: © luminaimages/Shutterstock, Alamy Images, Leonard Zhukovsky/Shutterstock, *bottom, left to right*: AP Images/Kiichiro Sato, Larry Luxner/Luxner News, Inc.; **82** The Granger Collection; **83** The Granger Collection; **84** *middle, left to right*: Kayte Deioma/PhotoEdit Inc., Simon Maina/Getty Images, Stephen McBrady/PhotoEdit Inc., *bottom, left to right*: Dave Schlabowske/Getty Images, Spencer Grant/PhotoEdit Inc.; **86** The Granger Collection; **91** *top left*: The Granger Collection, *top right*: Yale University Art Gallery, New Haven, CT, USA/The Bridgeman Art Library, *bottom left*: Hulton Archive/Getty Images, *bottom right*: Jean Leon Jerome Ferris (American, 1863–1930), "The First Thanksgiving", oil on canvas. Private Collection/The Bridgeman Art Library; **92** *top*: Discoro Teofilo de la Puebla Tolin (Brazilian, 1832–1901), "The First Landing of Christopher Columbus (1450-1506) in America", 1862, oil on canvas. Ayuntamiento de Coruna, Spain/The Bridgeman Art Library, *bottom*: Art Resource/The Metropolitan Museum of Art; **93** Bettman/Corbis; **96** *top*: Hulton Archive/Getty Images, *bottom*: Yale University Art Gallery, New Haven, CT, USA/The Bridgeman Art Library; **97** *top*: North Wind Picture Archives, *bottom left*: North Wind Picture Archives, *bottom right*: Bettman/Corbis; **102** Jean Leon Jerome Ferris (American, 1863-1930), "The First Thanksgiving", oil on canvas. Private Collection/The Bridgeman Art Library; **105** *top left*: A. Ramey/PhotoEdit Inc., *top right*: Ernst Wrba/Alamy Images, *bottom*: Mannie Garcia/Getty Images; **109** *top, left to right*: The Boston Tea Party, 16 December 1773: colored engraving, 19th century. The Granger Collection, New York, © Joseph Sohm; Visions of America/CORBIS, © Ariel Skelley/Corbis-NY, *bottom, left to right*: George Washington by Gilbert Stuart, Museum of the City of New York, "White House Historical Association (White House Collection)" 55, © Paul Freytag/zefa/ Corbis; **110** Currier & Ives, "Give Me Liberty or Give Me Death!", 1775. Lithograph, 1876. c. The Granger Collection, New York; **112** © Francis G. Mayer/CORBIS; **114** Corbis/Bettman; **116** © Joseph Sohm/Bettman/Corbis; **118** *top*: White House Historical Association, *bottom*: Tetra Images/Corbis; **119** © Ariel Skelley/Corbis-NY; **125** *top, left to right*: The Granger Collection, Kayte Deioma/PhotoEdit Inc., Stephen McBrady/PhotoEdit Inc., *bottom, left to right*: The Granger Collection, Simon Maina/Getty Images, Spencer Grant/PhotoEdit Inc.; **126** Corbis/Bettman; **128** Corbis/Bettman; **130** *top*: Library of Congress, *bottom, left to right*: Getty Images Inc-Taxi, Getty Images, Inc. Bridgeman, Getty Images Inc.-Hulton Archive Photos; **132** *top*: The Corcoran Gallery of Art/Corbis-NY, *bottom left*: Corbis, *bottom right*: Corbis/Bettman; **134** Xinhva/Alamy Stock Photo; **135** *left*: iStockphoto.com, *right*: Jonathan Ernst/Reuters/Alamy Stock Photo; **136** *top*: Getty Images Inc./Hulton Archive Photos, *bottom left*: iStockphoto.com, *bottom right*: AP Images/Pablo Martinez Monsivais; **138** The Granger Collection; **140** Peale, Charles Willson (1741–1827). (after): George Washington after the battle of Princeton, January 3, 1777. 1779. Oil on canvas, 234.5 x 155 cm. Inv.:MV 4560. Photo: Gerard Blot. Chateaux de Versailles et de Trianon, Versailles, France. Reunion des Musees Nationaux/Art Resource, NY; **145** *top left*: Library of Congress, *top right*: Corbis/Bettmann, *bottom left*: Corbis, *bottom right*: North Wind Picture Archives; **146** *top*: Library of Congress, *bottom left*: Print Collection. Miriam and Ira D. Wallach Division of Art, Prints and Photographs. The New York Public Library/Art Resource, NY. Astor, Lenox and Tilden Foundation, *bottom right*: CORBIS-NY; **147** *top*: © Michael W. Pendergrass/US Navy Photo/Reuters/Corbis-NY, *bottom*: Military History and Diplomacy Division, NMAH, Smithsonian Institution; **148** Mapresources.com; **150** *top*: Corbis, *bottom*: Corbis/Bettmann; **151** *top left*: Getty Images Inc.-Hulton Archive Photos, *top right*: © Collection of The New-York Historical Society. Negative number 37628, *bottom*: Corbis/Bettman; **152** *top*: Corbis/Bettmann, *bottom left*: Corbis, *bottom right*: Shutterstock; **155** North Wind Picture Archives; **156** *top, left to right*: Kayte Deioma/PhotoEdit Inc., Simon Maina/Getty Images, Stephen McBrady/PhotoEdit Inc, *bottom, left to right*: Dave Schlabowske/Getty Images, Spencer Grant/PhotoEdit Inc.; **157** *top left*: Associated Press, *top right*: Corbis, *bottom*: Corbis; **165** *top, left to right*: Corbis/Bettmann, Getty Images Inc.-Hulton Archive Photos, Jon Riley/Getty Images Inc.-Stone Allstock, *bottom, left to right*: Library of Congress, Corbis, AP Wide World Photos; **166** *top, left to right*: Corbis, Corbis, Getty Images-Hulton Archive Photos, *bottom, left to right*: Corbis, Getty Images Inc.-Hulton Archive Photos, Dorling Kindersley Media Library, Brown Brothers; **167** *top left*: Corbis, *top right*: © Lewis Hine/Corbis/Bettman, *bottom left*: Library of Congress, *bottom right*: Corbis; **168** Getty Images Inc.-Hulton Archive Photos; **170** *top*: Getty Images, Inc./Popperfoto, *middle*: Corbis, *bottom*: Corbis; **171** *top*: Corbis/Bettmann, *middle*: Corbis, *bottom*: Getty Images Inc.-Hulton Archive Photos; **172** *top*: Jon Riley/Getty Images Inc.-Stone Allstock, *middle*: Corbis, *bottom*: Black Star; **173** *top*: © Durand-Hudson-Langevin-Orban / Sygma / CORBIS All Rights Reserved, *middle, left to right*: Getty Images Inc./Popperfoto, Corbis, Corbis, *bottom, left to right*: Black Star, © Peter Turnley/Corbis; **176** AP Wide World Photos; **177** Corbis; **178** *left*: Aurora Photos, Inc., *right*: © Ron Crandall /The Image Works; **185** *top, left to right*: AP Wide World Photos, Zefa Visual Media-Germany/Corbis Zefa Collection, © Chris Aschenbrener/Alamy, *bottom, left to right*: Shutterstock, Nancy Alexander/PhotoEdit Inc., Tony Freeman/PhotoEdit Inc.; **186** *top row, left to right*: Rob Corbett/Alamy Images, Getty Images/Time Life Pictures, *row 2, left to right*: Andrew McCaul & Sarma Ozols/Alamy Images, Shutterstock, *row 3, left to right*: © Ariel Skelley/Corbis, Nancy Alexander/PhotoEdit Inc., *row 4, left to right*: Joe Sohm/Alamy Images, © Chris Aschenbrener/Alamy, *bottom, left to right*: Tony Freeman/PhotoEdit Inc., Tanya Constantine/Getty Images; **188** *top*: Corbis/Bettmann, *middle*: Getty Images Inc.-Hulton Archive Photos, *bottom*: White House Historical Association; **189** *top*: Getty Images, Inc. Bridgeman, *middle*: Corbis/Bettmann, *bottom*: Getty Images Inc.-Hulton Archive Photos; **190** *top*: Corbis/Bettmann, *middle*: © Corbis, *bottom*: Mark Shaw/MPTVIMAGES.COM; **191** *top*: Francis Miller/Getty Images/Time Life Pictures, *middle*: Corbis Digital Stock, *bottom*: © Corbis; **192** *top*: Getty Images Inc.-Hulton Archive Photos, *middle*: Corbis/Bettmann, *bottom*: Getty Images Inc.-Hulton Archive Photos; **193** *top*: Black Star, *bottom*: Allstar Picture Library/Alamy; **194** *top*: Pete Souza/Obama Transition Team/Handout/Corbis, *bottom*: Bastiaan Slabbers/Alamy Stock Photo; **199** *top, left to right*: Mikael Karlsson/Arresting Images, Ron Chapple/Taxi/Getty Images Inc., Stock Connection Blue/Alamy Stock Photo, *bottom, left to right*: iStockphoto.com, Tony Freeman/PhotoEdit Inc., Poster: Selective Service System/National Archives and Records Administration, Jim West/Alamy Stock Photo; **200** *top, left to right*: © Kayte Deioma/PhotoEdit Inc., Spencer Grant/PhotoEdit Inc., Stephen McBrady/PhotoEdit Inc., *middle, left to right*: Dave Schlabowske/Getty Images/Time Life Pictures, Shutterstock, *bottom, left to right*: Roberto Schmidt/Getty Images Inc.-Agence France Presse, Gary Miller/Getty Images-WireImage.com; **202** *top, left to right*: Mikael Karlsson/Arresting Images, iStockphoto.com, *bottom, left to right*: Tony Freeman/PhotoEdit Inc., Poster: Selective Service System/National Archives and Records Administration, Ron Chapple/Taxi/Getty Images Inc., Ron Chapple/taxi/Getty Images, Stock Connection Blue/Alamy Stock Photo; **204** *top, left to right*: Stock Connection Blue/Alamy Stock Photo, Win McNamee/Getty Images Inc.-Liaison, *row 2, left to right*: Chris Fitzgerald/The Image Works, © Joseph Sohm/Corbis, *row 3, left to right*: Scott J. Ferrell/Congressional Quarterly/Getty Images, Courtesy of the Office of Rep. Loretta Sanchez, © Syracuse Newspapers/Li-Hua Lan/The Image Works, *bottom, left to right*: J.D. Pooley/Getty Images Inc.-Liaison, © Marilyn Humphries/ The Image Works **206** *left*: Photolibrary.com, *right*: Ali Al-Saadi/Getty Images Inc.-Agence France Presse; **221**: David McNew/Getty Images, Inc.-Liaison; **222** SuperStock, Inc.

Welcome to the fourth edition of *Voices of Freedom*! This new full-color edition prepares students for the civics and English requirements of the new U.S. citizenship test and features activities designed to promote civic participation. The text also serves as a basic course for students in EL/Civics programs. It is designed for students at low-beginning, beginning, and low-intermediate levels whose limited language skills prevent them from using standard civics materials.

The text simultaneously develops students' civics knowledge and basic English skills. It introduces the required government and history topics through a research-based sequence of lessons that integrate a carefully controlled progression of grammar and vocabulary. This fourth edition includes many features specifically designed to prepare students for the new citizenship test and to promote active participation in class and in the community:

- Students practice the 100 official civics test questions throughout the text.
- Interview dialogs and civics test dialogs prepare students to communicate successfully during their appointment at the U.S. Citizenship and Immigration Services (USCIS) office.
- Unit tests include the required civics questions and the specific reading and writing test formats used in the citizenship exam.
- A new illustrated test-preparation section in the appendix walks students through the step-by-step procedures they will follow and the types of questions they will answer during their appointment at the USCIS office.
- Audio CDs included with the student text contain all readings, dialogs, the 100 civics questions, and listening comprehension activities.
- Civic participation activities include projects, issue discussions, and "online field trips" that enrich learning, promote student teamwork, and meet EL/Civics program goals.

In addition to the civics curriculum, *Voices of Freedom* prepares students to handle the give-and-take of interview questions about information on the N-400 citizenship application form since this is the basis for the USCIS officer's assessment of English language ability. This preparation includes critically important functional interview skills—communication strategies such as asking for repetition, asking for clarification, checking understanding, hesitating, and correcting.

Throughout the text, students also have many opportunities to share information about their native countries. In this way, *Voices of Freedom* aims to give respect and attention to each student's country, history, and culture as the student learns about the government, history, and civic life of the United States.

INSTRUCTIONAL FORMATS AND ACTIVITIES

Voices of Freedom lessons contain the following types of activities:

Vocabulary Previews: Picture dictionary lessons at the beginning of each unit introduce key vocabulary in a clear, easy-to-use format.

Readings: Basic information about government, history, and civics is introduced through short readings that are accompanied by one or more photographs. The readings are designed for high readability by low-level students. They are printed in large-size type, each sentence appears on a separate line, and there is very generous spacing between lines and between paragraphs.

Interview Dialogs and Civics Test Dialogs: Conversation practice activities provide students with authentic examples of the communication that occurs between a USCIS officer and a citizenship applicant during the interview. These dialogs cover a wide range of topics, including personal identification, personal information about background and family, and question-and-answer exchanges about government, history, and civics. The interview dialogs provide crucial practice since an applicant's English speaking ability is assessed through the normal course of the interview.

Check-Up Exercises: Workbook-style activities provide intensive skills practice in grammar, vocabulary, reading, and writing. Students need little or no teacher instruction or supervision to do these activities, so they are appropriate as homework or for use in class.

Civics Checks: The 100 official civics test questions are presented throughout the text in a chart format that enables students to easily practice alone or with a partner. Since many questions have multiple acceptable answers, students can choose to practice a single answer or to become familiar with alternative answers to a question.

Listening Exercises: Many units contain a listening activity, most of which require students to listen carefully for questions that sound the same or might otherwise be easily confused. Students learn to listen closely to avoid mistakes they might make during an interview due to their misunderstanding of a USCIS officer's question. All listening exercises are included on the Audio CDs. For the teacher, scripts for the listening exercises appear at the back of the textbook and in the Teacher's Guide.

"Questions & Answers" Activities: Unique lessons offer students important practice with the multiple ways a question might be posed by a USCIS officer. Students first study various ways that a particular question might be worded, and then they practice asking and answering questions with other students. In this way, students will not only know the answers, they will also "know the questions."

Review Lessons: At the end of many units, students do one or more review exercises. These serve to review the content of the unit and to cumulatively review content introduced earlier. Two unique formats for review activities are the "Information Exchange," in which students interview each other and record information collected during the interviews, and the "Talking Time Line," in which students match events with their dates, write the events on a time line, and then practice asking and answering questions based on the information.

Unit Tests: An assessment at the end of each unit evaluates student achievement of the learning objectives while developing the specific test-taking skills required for success during the English and civics exam. Each test contains the following: the official civics questions and answers that relate to a unit's content; a vocabulary activity in which students complete civics facts with words from the USCIS writing vocabulary list; and a reading and writing section where students read the types of questions and write from dictation the types of sentences that appear in the USCIS test. (Note: There are no multiple-choice items on the unit tests because that test-item format isn't used in the new citizenship exam.)

Unit Summaries: Lists of key unit vocabulary, grammar structures, and functional expressions appear at the end of each unit and serve as a convenient resource for review.

Civics Enrichment Activities: Activities at the end of each unit promote students' active participation in class and in the civic life of the community.

CIVIC PARTICIPATION ACTIVITIES bring civics instruction alive by involving students in local government through visits to city hall and representatives' offices, attendance at local government or school board meetings, and classroom visits by local officials.

PROJECT ACTIVITIES enable students to work together in teams or as a class to decorate bulletin boards with civics content, create local maps, simulate an Election Day in class, or have a Thanksgiving celebration.

COMMUNITY ISSUES DISCUSSIONS encourage students to apply civics content to their own lives, to identify issues and problems related to their well-being in the community, and to brainstorm solutions.

DEBATES organize students into teams, each team taking one side of an issue and arguing positions in front of the class.

INTERNET ACTIVITIES use online resources to take virtual field trips to historic places, to visit the web sites of government officials, and to do simple web-browsing tasks to find information.

The expanded Appendix provides several valuable resources:

On the Day of Your USCIS Interview, a helpful information section, reminds students about what they should bring to their appointment and offers practice checking in at the USCIS office.

The English Speaking Test Prep section prepares students to communicate successfully during all phases of their citizenship interview and exam— very important since the USCIS officer will evaluate the student's English speaking ability during the course of the interview. This section helps students practice how to greet the officer, how to engage in small talk while walking to the interview room, and how to provide or verify personal information that appears on the citizenship application. Students also learn how to ask for repetition and how to ask the officer to paraphrase a question they don't understand. This section also provides important practice with the challenging "Part 12" questions on the application form—the "Have you ever" questions that include difficult vocabulary and ask about sensitive subject matter such as criminal background, failure to pay taxes, and other issues that can jeopardize an application for citizenship.

Reading and Writing Test Prep sections provide the official vocabulary lists for the USCIS reading and writing tests. USCIS does not provide sample sentences for the tests, but these pages offer students practice with possible test sentences that appear in the textbook lessons.

The **100 Civics Test Questions** appear in a convenient chart format for easy review. The official USCIS English and Spanish versions of these questions and answers are presented side by side. Other language translations are available at www.uscis.gov.

The appendix also includes a comprehensive **Index** and a **Correlation Key** that provides a convenient reference for integrating the civics curriculum with lessons in English language programs including *Side by Side Plus*, *Word by Word*, and *Foundations*.

LOW BEGINNING-LEVEL STUDENTS

For students who are low-level beginners, the first two preparatory units of *Voices of Freedom* provide a basic foundation in English communication and literacy. The units introduce or review the alphabet, numbers, and basic vocabulary and expressions through the context of personal identification skills, in a sequence that is appropriate for low beginners. The easy exercise formats are designed to give these students a feeling of immediate success and momentum in their study of English and Civics. Students who already have some basic understanding of English can skip these preparatory units and begin their studies with Unit 1.

TEACHING TECHNIQUES

Voices of Freedom has been designed for ease-of-use for the teacher as well as the students. Teachers should feel encouraged to use the text's activities in the way that is most appropriate for their teaching styles and the needs and learning styles of their students.

Three of the central learning devices in the text are the readings, the Civics Check question-and-answer charts, and the dialogs (the Interview and Civics Test conversations). For these three types of activities, teachers may want to use or adapt the following suggestions:

Readings

1. Have students talk about the photograph and/or their own experiences in order to establish a context, or schema, for what they are about to read.

2. Have students read silently. (If you wish, you may read the passage aloud or play the audio program as they read silently.)

3. Ask students a simple question about each line of the reading. For low beginners, ask the questions in the sequence of the reading. For higher-level students, you might want to ask the questions out of sequence.

4. Ask students if they don't understand any vocabulary. Have students help define any unfamiliar words.

5. Do a choral repetition of the reading, line by line. (This is not reading practice, but rather is speaking practice—appropriate since most of the reading content in *Voices of Freedom* is the basis for the conversation practice that follows.)

6. Class Circle Reading: Have students read the passage as a class with different students reading each line in turn. You can assign who will read in a variety of ways: by seating patterns, by calling on students, or by letting students take turns spontaneously.

7. Pair Practice: Have students work in pairs, reading the passage to each other paragraph by paragraph, for further speaking practice. Circulate around the room, checking students' reading and pronunciation, and focus attention on students who need more assistance.

8. When comprehension questions about a reading appear in the "Check-Up" exercises that follow, have students first write their answers and then practice in pairs asking and answering these questions aloud.

Civics Check Question & Answer Charts

The chart format for presentation of the 100 official civics test questions enables students to easily practice in class, with a study partner outside of class, or alone with the audio. In class, students can practice in a variety of ways:

PAIR PRACTICE: Have students work in pairs, taking turns asking and answering the questions.

LINE PRACTICE: Have students stand in two lines facing each other. Each pair of facing students should take turns asking and answering a question. After sufficient time for this practice, say "Move," and have one line of students move down one position while the other line remains in place. (The student at the end of the line moves to the beginning of the line.) In this way, new pairs are created and students practice with another partner. Continue until students have practiced all the questions.

"ROUND ROBIN": Have students circulate around the room and ask each other the questions. Students should move on to another person after they have taken turns asking and answering a question.

This classroom practice will prepare students to extend learning outside of class by working with a study partner. Students can also practice alone, reading the questions in the left column while covering the answers in the right column and then checking their answers. (Note: Since many questions have multiple acceptable answers, you might encourage low beginners to consistently practice a single answer to a question, while higher-level students can practice the multiple answers.)

Interview Dialogs and Civics Test Dialogs

1. Set the scene. Have students look at the photograph and decide who the people are. You might simply mention in a word or two what they are talking about, such as "the person's address" or "the flag."

2. Have students listen to the dialog with their books closed. Present the dialog yourself (taking both roles), present it with the help of another student, have two students present it to the rest of the class, or play the audio. (If a dialog line has a blank and an answer-choice box, use the first answer to complete the line. The audio always contains the first answer.)

3. Choral Repetition: Have students repeat each line of the dialog in unison after you. (Books still closed.)

4. Have students open their books and look at the dialog. Ask if there are any questions about vocabulary.

5. Choral Conversation Practice:

   a. Divide the class into two groups (two halves or by rows). Have Group 1 say Speaker A's lines in unison, and have Group 2 say Speaker B's lines. Then reverse.

and/or

   b. Say Speaker A's lines and have the entire class say Speaker B's lines in unison. Then reverse.

6. Call on one or two pairs of students to present the dialog.

7. Pair Practice: Have students practice the dialog in pairs, taking turns being Speaker A and Speaker B. Encourage students to look at each other during the practice rather than "burying" their heads in the books. This will help their spoken language sound more authentic and conversational.

   (You can pair students in different ways. You can pair students of similar ability together and thereby focus your attention on those pairs of students who require more attention. Or you can pair weaker students with stronger ones so that your more capable students have the opportunity to consolidate their skills while providing help to others in the class.)

8. New Dialogs: In Units A and B, the Interview dialogs are followed by "skeletal" dialogs with blank lines. Have students insert their own information and practice new conversations.

(Note: In Units 1–12, many Civics Test dialogs have blank lines and answer-choice boxes since many questions have multiple acceptable answers. You might encourage low beginners to consistently practice the first answer to a question, while higher-level students can practice the multiple answers. The audio always contains the first answer.)

A FINAL WORD: THE GOAL OF CIVICS EDUCATION

A century ago, the goal of citizenship education in so-called "Americanization" classes was to indoctrinate students with U.S. civics information in a way that often discredited their native countries and cultures. It was as though students had to renounce their backgrounds and heritages in order to acquire knowledge about their new country. Now we aspire to a nobler effort: to offer students the language skills and civics knowledge they need to attain citizenship, to live full and productive lives, and to participate fully in the civic life of their communities and the country, and to do so through an educational program that recognizes and respects the diversity of cultures, histories, and experiences that our students bring to our classrooms . . . and the nation.

Bill Bliss

PERSONAL INFORMATION
IDENTIFICATION CARDS
ALPHABET
NUMBERS

- **To Be**
- **WH-Questions**

VOCABULARY PREVIEW

PERMANENT RESIDENT CARD

① NAME RIVERA, CARLOS M.

INS A# A92475816

Birthdate 03/17/76　Category IR6　Sex M

Country of Birth Mexico

CARD EXPIRES 06/29/12

Resident Since 11/17/01

C1USA0924758166EAC0013440673<<
0612029M1004268MEX<<<<<<<<<<0
RIVERA<<CARLOS<<<<<<<<<<<<<<<<

SOCIAL SECURITY

408-37-1692

THIS NUMBER HAS BEEN ESTABLISHED FOR

CARLOS M. RIVERA

Carlos M. Rivera
SIGNATURE

1. permanent resident card
2. last name / family name / surname
3. first name / given name
4. middle initial
5. A-number
6. social security card
7. social security number
8. signature

Permanent Resident Card

CD 1: Track 3

My name is Carlos Rivera.
I'm a permanent resident.
This is my permanent resident card.

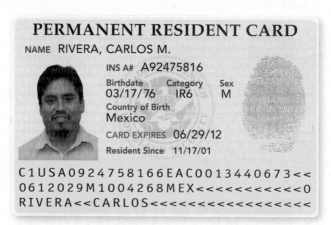

My last name* is Rivera.
My first name† is Carlos.
My middle name is Manuel.
My full name is Carlos Manuel Rivera.

I'm applying for citizenship.
I want to be a citizen of the United States of America.

* last name = family name
            surname

† first name = given name

Vocabulary Check

| card | citizen | citizenship | first | last | name |

1. My _____name_____ is Carlos Rivera.

2. My _____ name is Rivera.

3. My _____ name is Carlos.

4. I want to be a _____.

5. This is my permanent resident _____.

6. I'm applying for _____.

Grammar Check

1. My first name   be (is)   Carlos.

2. [My   I'm] a permanent resident.

3. [My   I'm] last name is Rivera.

4. [I   I'm] applying for citizenship.

5. I want to [am   be] a citizen.

Writing: *What's Your Name?*

1. _____ _____ _____
   First Name   Middle Name   Last Name

2. _____ _____ _____
   Last Name   First Name   Middle Name

3. _____
   (Family Name) (Given Name) (Middle Name)

4.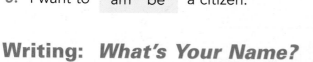
   Surname   First Name   Full Middle Name

The Alphabet

Aa Bb Cc Dd Ee Ff Gg Hh Ii Jj Kk Ll Mm
Nn Oo Pp Qq Rr Ss Tt Uu Vv Ww Xx Yy Zz

Practice with another student.

CD 1: Track 5

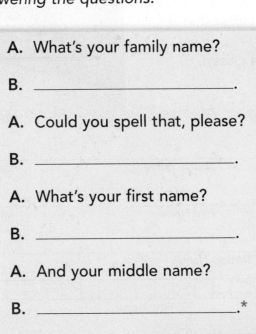

A. What's your family name?

B. Rivera.

A. Could you spell that, please?

B. R-I-V-E-R-A.

A. What's your first name?

B. Carlos.

A. And your middle name?

B. Manuel.

Now practice new conversations with other students. Use your information. Take turns asking and answering the questions.

A. What's your family name?

B. _____.

A. Could you spell that, please?

B. _____.

A. What's your first name?

B. _____.

A. And your middle name?

B. _____.*

* If no middle name, say, "I don't have a middle name."

Alphabet Practice

Fill in the missing letters of the alphabet. Then use the letters to make a word.

1. A B C D E F G H I J K L M N O P Q R S T U V W X Y Z
   N A M E

2. ☐ B ☐ ☐ E F G H I J K L M N O P Q ☐ S T U V W X Y Z
   ☐ ☐ ☐ ☐

3. ☐ B C D E F G H I J K ☐ M N O P Q R ☐ ☐ U V W X Y Z
   ☐ ☐ ☐ ☐

4. ☐ B C D E ☐ G H ☐ J K ☐ ☐ N O P Q R S T U V W X ☐ Z
   ☐ ☐ ☐ ☐ ☐

CD 1: Track 6

Listening

Listen and circle the correct answer.

1. (Martinez)   Ramirez

2. Garcia   Garza

3. Ly   Le

4. Moreno   Romero

5. Wang   Wong

6. Mansoor   Mansour

Writing: *Fill Out the Form*

Part 2. Information About You *(Person applying for naturalization)*

1. **Your Current Legal Name** *(do not provide a nickname)*

Family Name *(Last Name)*	Given Name *(First Name)*	Middle Name *(if applicable)*

2. **Your Name Exactly As It Appears on Your Permanent Resident Card** *(if applicable)*

Family Name *(Last Name)*	Given Name *(First Name)*	Middle Name *(if applicable)*

0	zero
1	one
2	two
3	three
4	four
5	five
6	six
7	seven
8	eight
9	nine

CD 1: Track 7

CD 1: Track 8

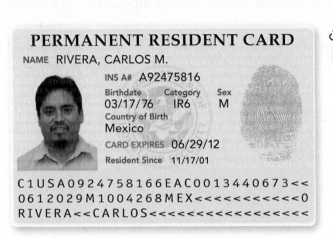

This is my permanent resident card.
My A-number is A-92475816.

This is my social security card.
My social security number is 408-37-1692.*

RIVERA Carlos M 80 Stanley Av
Los Angeles **213 257-9108**

This is my telephone number.
My telephone number is (213) 257-9108.

* 0 = "zero" or "oh"

Matching

__c__ 1. name   **a.** A-92475816

____ 2. telephone number   **b.** 408-37-1692

____ 3. social security number   **c.** Carlos Rivera

____ 4. A-number   **d.** (213) 257-9108

Answer These Questions

1. What's your A-number?   A– _ _ _ _ _ _ _ _ _

2. What's your social security number?   _ _ _ - _ _ - _ _ _ _

3. What's your home telephone number?
   (Include area code)   (_ _ _) _ _ _ - _ _ _ _

4. What's your phone number at work?
   (Include area code)   (_ _ _) _ _ _ - _ _ _ _

Writing: *Fill Out the Form*

Enter Your 9 Digit A-Number: ▶ A- [ ][ ][ ][ ][ ][ ][ ][ ][ ]	U.S. Social Security Number *(if applicable)* [ ][ ][ ][ ][ ][ ][ ][ ][ ]

Part 2. Information About You *(Person applying for naturalization)*

1. **Your Current Legal Name** (*do not* provide a nickname)

Family Name *(Last Name)*	Given Name *(First Name)*	Middle Name *(if applicable)*

2. **Your Name Exactly As It Appears on Your Permanent Resident Card** *(if applicable)*

Family Name *(Last Name)*	Given Name *(First Name)*	Middle Name *(if applicable)*

Part 3. Information to Contact You

1. **Daytime Phone Number** ([ ][ ][ ]) [ ][ ][ ] - [ ][ ][ ][ ]	2. **Work Phone Number** *(if any)* ([ ][ ][ ]) [ ][ ][ ] - [ ][ ][ ][ ]	3. **Evening Phone Number** ([ ][ ][ ]) [ ][ ][ ] - [ ][ ][ ][ ]
4. **Mobile Phone Number** *(if any)* ([ ][ ][ ]) [ ][ ][ ] - [ ][ ][ ][ ]	5. **E-mail Address** *(if any)*	

10	ten
11	eleven
12	twelve
13	thirteen
14	fourteen
15	fifteen
16	sixteen
17	seventeen
18	eighteen
19	nineteen
20	twenty
30	thirty
40	forty
50	fifty
60	sixty
70	seventy
80	eighty
90	ninety

My address is 80 Stanley Avenue.
My apartment number is 12-D.
The name of my city is Los Angeles.
The name of my state is California.
California is in the United States of America.
My zip code is 90048.

Your Information

My address is _____.

(My apartment number is _____.)

The name of my city is _____.

The name of my state is _____.

_____ is in the United States of America.

My zip code is _____.

8

Matching

<u>d</u>   1.   phone number   a.   Los Angeles

_____   2.   state   b.   12-D

_____   3.   zip code   c.   80 Stanley Avenue

_____   4.   city   d.   (213) 257-9108

_____   5.   address   e.   90048

_____   6.   apartment number   f.   California

Reading Addresses

80 Stanley Avenue	**eighty**
1628 Donaldson Street	**sixteen twenty-eight**
214 Conway Avenue	{ **two fourteen** / **two hundred and fourteen** }

Say these addresses.

13 Stanley Avenue   4826 Greenwood Avenue

60 Spring Street   549 Parkman Avenue

1360 Donaldson Street   842 Main Street

Listening

CD 1: Track 11

Listen and circle the number you hear.

1.   60   (30)   4.   4256   4615

2.   13   19   5.   1839   3918

3.   15   50   6.   482   842

Practice with another student.

A. What's your USCIS file number?

B. You mean my A-number?

A. Yes.

B. It's A-92475816.

A. What's your home telephone number including area code?

B. 213-257-9108.

A. What's your address?

B. 80 Stanley Avenue, apartment 12-D, Los Angeles, California.

A. And your zip code?

B. 90048.

Now practice new conversations with other students. Use your information. Take turns asking and answering the questions.

A. What's your USCIS file number?

B. You mean my A-number?

A. Yes.

B. It's A-_____.

A. What's your home telephone number including area code?

B. _____.

A. What's your address?

B. _____.

A. And your zip code?

B. _____.

Check-Up

Questions and Answers

Read these questions and answer them.

What's your family name?
(Could you spell that, please?)
What's your first name?
What's your middle name?
What's your home address?
What's your apartment number?
What's the name of your city?
What's the name of your county?
What's the name of your state?
What's your zip code?
What's your daytime telephone number including area code?
What's your eveing telephone number including area code?
What's your A-number?

Now use these questions to interview another student.

Writing: *Fill Out the Form*

Family Name *(Last Name)*

Given Name *(First Name)*   Middle Name *(If applicable)*

Street Number and Name   Apt. Ste. Flr.   Number

City   County   State   Zip Code + 4

Daytime Phone Number   Evening Phone Number   E-Mail Address *(If any)*
(   )   (   )

U.S. Social Security Number   Enter Your 9 Digit A-Number
                                A-

Civics Enrichment

Civic Participation

Discuss: A permanent resident card and a social security card are forms of personal identification. What are other forms of personal identification? Which do you have? Why are forms of personal identification important? Where do you get them?

Project

Make a list of emergency telephone numbers for your community: Police, Fire, Ambulance, Poison Control Center. Make copies. Put a list next to each telephone where you live.

Community Issues

Discuss: Is it difficult to use emergency services in your community? Why?

UNIT SUMMARY

KEY VOCABULARY

PERSONAL INFORMATION

address
apartment number
area code
avenue
city
country
county
e-mail address
family name
file number
first name
full name
given name
home address
last name
middle name
name
number
phone number
social security number
state
street
surname
telephone number
zip code

IDENTIFICATION CARDS

A-number
card
permanent resident card
social security card
USCIS A-number
USCIS file number

IMMIGRATION STATUS

citizen
citizenship
permanent resident

ACTIONS

apply
spell
want (to)
write

OTHER WORDS

a
am
and
capital letters
daytime
evening
for
from
I
include
including
is
my
of
please
that
the
this
United States of America
what
work
yes
your

NUMBERS

0	zero (oh)
1	one
2	two
3	three
4	four
5	five
6	six
7	seven
8	eight
9	nine
10	ten
11	eleven
12	twelve
13	thirteen
14	fourteen
15	fifteen
16	sixteen
17	seventeen
18	eighteen
19	nineteen
20	twenty
30	thirty
40	forty
50	fifty
60	sixty
70	seventy
80	eighty
90	ninety

GRAMMAR

To Be

My name **is** Carlos Rivera.
I'm a permanent resident.

WH-Questions

What's your family name?

FUNCTIONAL EXPRESSIONS

Clarifying

Could you spell that, please?
You mean . . . ?

PERSONAL INFORMATION
MONTHS OF THE YEAR
DATES

- **To Be**
- **WH-Questions**
- **Yes/No Questions**
- **Short Answers**

VOCABULARY PREVIEW

CD 1: Track 13

1 JAN

2 FEB

3 MAR

4 APR

5 MAY

6 JUN

7 JUL

8 AUG

9 SEP

10 OCT

11 NOV

12 DEC

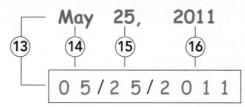

May 25, 2011

13 **14** **15** **16**

0 5 / 2 5 / 2 0 1 1

1. January	5. May	9. September	13. date
2. February	6. June	10. October	14. month
3. March	7. July	11. November	15. day
4. April	8. August	12. December	16. year

CD 1: Track 14

My name is Maria Lopez.
I'm from Mexico.
Now I'm a permanent resident of the United States.
The name of my city is Houston.
Houston is in the state of Texas.

I'm Mexican.
I was born in Monterrey.
Monterrey is in the state of Nuevo León.
Nuevo León is a state in Mexico.

I was born on May 4, 1979.
My mother's name is Gloria.
My father's name is Oscar.
My mother and father are in Monterrey.

I'm applying for naturalization.*
I want to be a citizen of the United States.

* naturalization = citizenship

Check-Up

Matching

<u>d</u> 1. My name is

____ 2. I'm

____ 3. I was born in

____ 4. I was born on

____ 5. I'm applying for

a. Monterrey.

b. naturalization.

c. Mexican.

d. Maria Lopez.

e. May 4, 1979.

Vocabulary Check

born	city	mother	name	state

1. My _____<u>name</u>_____ is Maria Lopez.

2. The name of my _____ is Houston.

3. The name of my _____ is Texas.

4. I was _____ in Monterrey.

5. My father and _____ are in Monterrey.

Fill Out the Form

October 21, 2010   10/21/2010
May 4, 1979   05/04/1979

Date of Birth *(mm/dd/yyyy)*

Country of Birth

Sharing

Bring in photographs of people in your family. Tell about them.

This is my _____.

His/Her name is _____.

He/She is in _____.
              (where?)

Family Members		
mother	daughter	aunt
father	son	uncle
wife	sister	grandmother
husband	brother	grandfather

What's Your Place of Birth?

CD 1: Track 15

Practice with another student.

A. What's your place of birth?

B. Excuse me?

A. Where were you born?
What's your native country?

B. I was born in Mexico.

A. In what city or town?

B. I was born in Monterrey.

A. Where is that?

B. Monterrey is in the state of Nuevo León.

Now practice new conversations with other students. Use your information. Take turns asking and answering the questions.

A. What's your place of birth?

B. Excuse me?

A. Where were you born? What's your native country?

B. I was born in _____.

A. In what city or town?

B. I was born in _____.

A. Where is that?

B. _____ is in _____.

Check-Up

Questions and Answers

Practice the different ways to ask these questions.

What's your nationality?	I'm **Mexican**.
What's your place of birth? What's your country of birth? What's your native country? What country are you from? Where were you born? Where are you from?	**Mexico**.
In what city or town were you born? What city or town were you born in? Where were you born?	I was born in **Monterrey**.

Now answer these questions.

1. What's your nationality?
2. What's your country of birth?
3. In what city or town were you born?

Grammar Check

Where	What

1. ___What___ is your nationality?

2. _____ were you born?

3. _____ country are you from?

4. _____ city or town were you born in?

5. _____ are you from?

Listening

CD 1: Track 16

*On Line **A**, write your **place** of birth. On Line **B**, write your **date** of birth.*

A. _____	B. _____

*Now listen and circle **A** or **B**.*

1. (A) B   3.   A   B   5.   A   B

2. A   B   4.   A   B   6.   A   B

What's Your Date of Birth?

Practice with another student.

A. What's your date of birth?

B. I'm sorry. I didn't understand.
   Could you please say that again?

A. When were you born?

B. I was born on May 4, 1979.

A. On May 4, 1979?

B. Yes. That's right.

*Now practice new conversations with other students. Use your information.
Take turns asking and answering the questions.*

A. What's your date of birth?

B. I'm sorry. I didn't understand. Could you please say that again?

A. When were you born?

B. I was born on _____.

A. On _____?

B. Yes. That's right.

Months and Years

Practice the months of the year.

January	April	July	October
February	May	August	November
March	June	September	December

Practice reading the years.

1979	nineteen seventy-nine
1776	seventeen seventy-six
2010	two thousand ten

Questions and Answers

Practice the different ways to ask these questions.

What year were you born? In what year were you born?	I was born in 1979.
In what month were you born?	I was born in May.
What's your date of birth? What's your birth date? When were you born?	I was born on May 4, 1979.

Now answer these questions.

1. What year were you born? _____

2. In what month were you born? _____

3. What's your date of birth? _____

Calendar Activity

Bring in a calendar that you can write on. Ask other students, "When were you born?" Write their birthdays on the calendar. Then, discuss other important dates, such as U.S. holidays and native country holidays. Add these dates to the calendar.

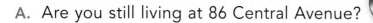

Practice with another student.

CD 1: Track 18

A. Are you still living at 86 Central Avenue?

B. Yes, I am.

A. And is your zip code 10715?

B. Yes, it is.

A. Are you still living at 65 Main Street?

B. No, I'm not.

A. 65 Main Street isn't your current address?

B. No, it isn't. My new address is 1247 Washington Street in Arlington.

A. And what's the zip code?

B. 22215.

Now practice new conversations with other students. Use the dialog that fits your situation. Take turns asking and answering the questions.

A. Are you still living at _____?

B. Yes, I am.

A. And is your zip code _____?

B. Yes, it is.

A. Are you still living at _____?

B. No, I'm not.

A. _____ isn't your current address?

B. No, it isn't. My new address is _____

in _____.

A. And what's the zip code?

B. _____.

INTERVIEW | Let Me Verify Some Information

Practice with another student.

A. Let me verify some information. Your family name is Garcia. Is that right?

B. Yes, it is.

A. And your first name is Victor. Is that correct?

B. No, it isn't. My first name is Francisco. My MIDDLE name is Victor.

A. I see. Your nationality is Mexican?

B. Yes. That's right.

A. Is your date of birth November 20, 1975?

B. No. That's not correct. My date of birth is OCTOBER 20, 1975.

A. All right. And on what date did you become a permanent resident?

B. On April 10, 2003.

Now practice new conversations with other students. Use your information.
Take turns asking and answering the questions.

A. Let me verify some information. Your family name is _____. Is that right?

B. Yes, it is.

A. And your first name is _____. Is that correct?

B. No, it isn't. My first name is _____.

   My MIDDLE name is _____.

A. I see. Your nationality is _____?

B. Yes. That's right.

A. Is your date of birth _____?

B. No. That's not correct. My date of birth is _____.

A. All right. And on what date did you become a permanent resident?

B. On _____.

21

Check-Up

Questions and Answers

Practice the different ways to ask and answer these questions.

> Is your family name Garcia?
> Your family name is Garcia. Is that right?
> Your family name is Garcia. Is that correct?
> Your family name is Garcia?
>
> | Yes. | No. |
> |---|---|
> | Yes, it is. | No, it isn't. |
> | Yes. That's correct. | No. That's not correct. |
> | Yes. That's right. | No. That's not right. |

Now answer these questions.

1. Your native country is Mexico. Is that right?
2. Your telephone number is 241-6289. Is that correct?
3. Is your home in Los Angeles?
4. Your nationality is Chinese?

Writing: *Fill Out the Form*

Part 2. Information About You *(continued)*   A- ☐☐☐☐☐☐☐☐☐

5. **U.S. Social Security Number**
   (if applicable)

   ☐☐☐☐☐☐☐☐☐

6. **Date of Birth**
   (mm/dd/yyyy)

   ▶ ☐

7. **Date You Became a Permanent Resident**
   (mm/dd/yyyy)

   ▶ ☐

8. **Country of Birth**

   ☐

9. **Country of Citizenship or Nationality**

   ☐

Part 3. Information to Contact You

1. **Daytime Phone Number**
   (☐☐☐) ☐☐☐ - ☐☐☐☐

2. **Work Phone Number** *(if any)*
   (☐☐☐) ☐☐☐ - ☐☐☐☐

3. **Evening Phone Number**
   (☐☐☐) ☐☐☐ - ☐☐☐☐

4. **Mobile Phone Number** *(if any)*
   (☐☐☐) ☐☐☐ - ☐☐☐☐

5. **E-mail Address** *(if any)*
   ☐

Information Exchange

Read these questions and answer them.

> What's your name?
>
> (Could you spell that, please?)
>
> What's your nationality?
>
> What country are you from?
>
> In what city or town were you born?
>
> What's your date of birth?

Now use these questions to interview other students. Write the information below.

	Name	Nationality	Country	City or Town	Date of Birth
1.					
2.					
3.					
4.					
5.					
6.					

Additional Practice

Practice with other students. Take turns asking and answering these questions.

1. What's the name of your state?
2. What's the name of your city?
3. What's your home address including apartment number?
4. What's your zip code?
5. What's your home telephone number including area code?
6. What's your work phone number including area code?
7. What's your nationality?
8. What's your country of birth?
9. In what city or town were you born?

Civics Enrichment

As a class, go around your school and introduce yourselves to the people in the office, the library, and other places. Tell your name, your nationality, where you were born, when you came to the United States, and other information.

Bulletin Board Project: Bring in a map of your native country. Show students the city or town where you were born. Write a paragraph about yourself. Tell your name, your nationality, your country of birth, and the city or town where you were born. As a class, make a bulletin board display of student maps and paragraphs. Use string to connect students' places of birth on the maps to the paragraphs.

Calendar Project: As a class, make a calendar of all the months you will study together. On the calendar, write student birthdays, U.S. holidays, native country holidays, and other special dates. Hang the calendar on a wall or bulletin board.

UNIT SUMMARY

KEY VOCABULARY

PERSONAL INFORMATION

address	home address
apartment number	home telephone number
area code	information
birth	middle name
birth date	name
born	nationality
city	native country
country	place of birth
country of birth	social security number
country of nationality	state
current address	street
date	telephone number
date of birth	town
e-mail address	work phone number
family name	zip code
first name	

FAMILY MEMBERS

aunt
brother
daughter
father
grandfather
grandmother
husband
mother
sister
son
uncle
wife

TIME EXPRESSIONS

date
day
month
year

MONTHS

January
February
March
April
May
June
July
August
September
October
November
December

IMMIGRATION STATUS

citizen
citizenship
naturalization
permanent resident

GRAMMAR

TO BE

My name **is** Maria Lopez.
I'm from Mexico.
My mother and father **are** in Monterrey.

WH-QUESTIONS

What's your place of birth?
Where were you born?
When were you born?

YES/NO QUESTIONS

Are you still living at 86 Central Avenue?
Is your zip code 10715?

SHORT ANSWERS

Yes, I am.
No, I'm not.
Yes, it is.
No, it isn't.

FUNCTIONAL EXPRESSIONS

ASKING FOR REPETITION

Excuse me?
Could you please say that again?

CLARIFYING

On *May 4, 1979*?

EXPRESSING LACK OF UNDERSTANDING

I'm sorry. I didn't understand.

VERIFYING INFORMATION

Is that right?
Is that correct?
　　Yes. That's right.
　　No. That's not correct.

MAPS & GEOGRAPHY
STATES & CAPITALS
FAMOUS U.S. LANDMARKS
U.S. TERRITORIES

- **To Be**
- **WH-Questions**
- **Yes/No Questions**
- **Short Answers**

VOCABULARY PREVIEW

CD 1: Track 20

1. Canada
2. the United States
3. Mexico
4. Washington, D.C.
5. Pacific Ocean
6. Atlantic Ocean
7. north
8. south
9. west
10. east

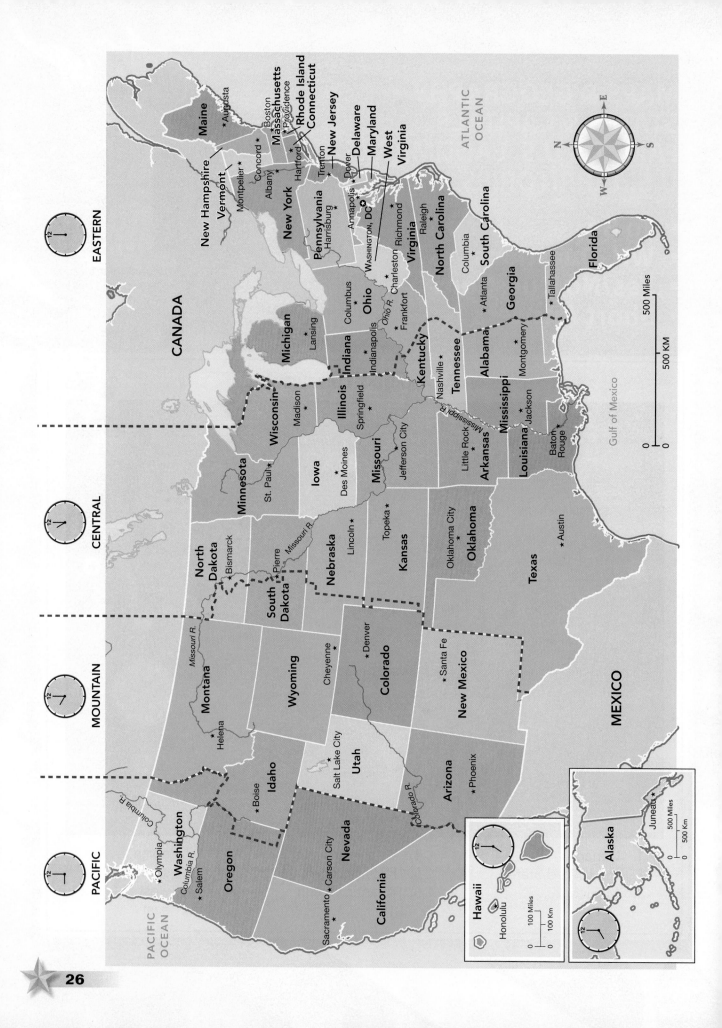

The United States is a large country.
The United States is between two other countries.
Canada is north of the United States.
Mexico is south of the United States.

Many states border Canada: Maine, New Hampshire, Vermont,
    New York, Pennsylvania, Ohio, Michigan, Minnesota,
    North Dakota, Montana, Idaho, Washington, and Alaska.

Four states border Mexico: California, Arizona, New Mexico, and
    Texas.

The United States is between two oceans.
The Atlantic Ocean is on the East Coast of the United States.
The Pacific Ocean is on the West Coast of the United States.

The longest river in the United States is the Missouri River.
The second longest river is the Mississippi River.

The capital of the United States is Washington, D.C.

Map Activity

What's the name of your state?
Point to your state on the map.

What's the name of your state capital?
Point to your state capital on the map.

What's the name of the capital of the United States?
Point to the capital of the United States on the map.

Vocabulary Check

north	south	east	west	capital	country

1. The United States is a large _____ country _____.

2. Canada is _____ of the United States.

3. The _____ of the United States is Washington, D.C.

4. The Atlantic Ocean is _____ of the United States.

5. The Pacific Ocean is _____ of the United States.

6. Mexico is _____ of the United States.

Grammar Check

> Yes, it is.
> No, it isn't.

1. Is the United States a large country? _____ Yes, it is. _____

2. Is the capital of the United States in California? _____

3. Is Canada north of the United States? _____

4. Is the Atlantic Ocean on the West Coast of the United States? _____

5. Is the United States between Canada and Mexico? _____

6. Is Washington, D.C. the capital of the United States? _____

Map Game

Think of a state and have other students guess it. Give them clues. Use the words *north*, *south*, *east*, and *west*. Give clues one at a time until the students guess correctly. For example: "I'm thinking of a state that's east of Arizona," "It's west of Louisiana," and so on.

Civics Check

*Practice the questions and answers.**

1.	What ocean is on the West Coast of the United States?	The Pacific Ocean
2.	What ocean is on the East Coast of the United States?	The Atlantic Ocean
3.	What is the capital of the United States?	Washington, D.C.
4.	Name one state that borders Canada.	Maine Minnesota New Hampshire North Dakota Vermont Montana New York Idaho Pennsylvania Washington Ohio Alaska Michigan
5.	Name one state that borders Mexico.	California New Mexico Arizona Texas
6.	Name one of the two longest rivers in the United States.	The Missouri River The Mississippi River

* Some questions have more than one possible answer. Only one answer is required unless the question asks for more.

Map Discussion

Where did you first enter the United States?
Do you have any friends or family members in other states? Where?
Which states do you want to visit? Why?

Your Native Country

Answer these questions.

1. What's the name of your native country? _____

2. What's the capital of your native country? _____

3. What city or town are you from? _____

4. What is north of your native country? south? east? west?

_____

_____

Draw a map of your native country. On the map, show the capital, show your city or town, and show what is north, south, east, and west of your native country.

CD 1: Track 23

The Statue of Liberty is in New York.

It is on an island in New York Harbor.

New York Harbor borders the states of New York and New Jersey.

It is at the southern end of the Hudson River.

The Statue of Liberty is a symbol of American freedom.

There are many other famous landmarks in the United States.

The Washington Monument is in Washington, D.C.

The Liberty Bell is in Philadelphia, Pennsylvania.

The Golden Gate Bridge is in San Francisco, California.

Mount Rushmore is in Keystone, South Dakota.

The Alamo is in San Antonio, Texas.

Grand Canyon National Park is in Arizona.

The Gateway Arch is on the Mississippi River in St. Louis, Missouri.

The Hollywood sign is in Hollywood, California.

Map Activity

Look at the map on page 26. Point to the states where these landmarks are located.

Some places are territories of the United States.

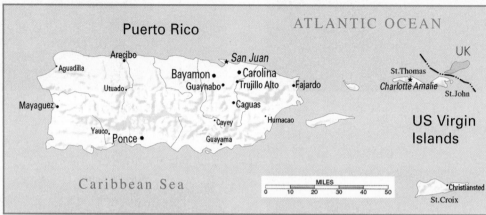

Puerto Rico is an island in the Caribbean.
It is between the Caribbean Sea and the Atlantic Ocean.

The U.S. Virgin Islands is a group of three islands in the Caribbean.

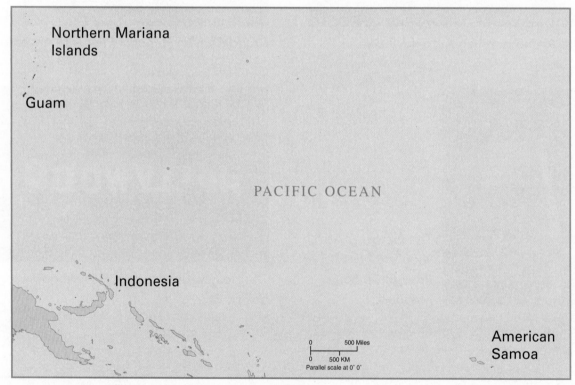

The Northern Mariana Islands are in the western Pacific Ocean.

Guam is an island in the western Pacific Ocean.
It is the western-most territory of the United States.

American Samoa is a group of six islands in the South Pacific.

Vocabulary Check

Canyon	Coast	Harbor	Islands	Ocean	River

1. The Gateway Arch is on the Mississippi _____ River _____.

2. The Statue of Liberty is in New York _____.

3. Grand _____ National Park is in Arizona.

4. Guam is in the western Pacific _____.

5. The U.S. Virgin _____ is a territory of the United States.

6. The Atlantic Ocean is on the East _____ of the United States.

Civics Check

CD 1: Track 25

*Practice the questions and answers.**

1.	Where is the Statue of Liberty?	New York New York Harbor Liberty Island (New Jersey)** (Near New York City)** (On the Hudson River)** (** also acceptable answers)
2.	Name one U.S. territory.	Puerto Rico The U.S. Virgin Islands American Samoa The Northern Mariana Islands Guam
3.	What is the capital of the United States?	Washington, D.C.
4.	What ocean is on the East Coast of the United States?	The Atlantic Ocean
5.	What ocean is on the West Coast of the United States?	The Pacific Ocean

* Some questions have more than one possible answer. Only one answer is required unless the question asks for more.

A Landmark in Your Native Country

Describe a famous landmark in your native country. Where is it? Why is it famous? If you have a picture of this landmark or a book about it, bring it to class and share with other students.

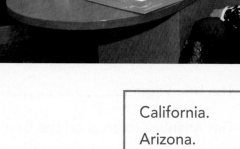

Practice with other students. Take turns asking and answering the questions.

A. Are you ready for some civics questions?

B. Yes.

A. Name one state that borders Mexico.

B. I'm sorry. Please repeat the question.

A. Okay. Name one state that borders Mexico.

B. _____ *

A. That's correct.

> California.
> Arizona.
> New Mexico.
> Texas.

A. What ocean is on the West Coast of the United States?

B. I'm sorry. Did you say the West Coast?

A. Yes. The West Coast.

B. _____ *

A. That's right.

> The Pacific Ocean.
> The Pacific.

A. What ocean is on the East Coast of the United States?

B. I'm sorry. Did you say the West Coast?

A. No. The *East* Coast.

B. _____ *

A. Very good.

> The Atlantic Ocean.
> The Atlantic.

* This question has more than one possible answer. Only one answer is required during the citizenship exam.

CD 1: Tracks 27–28

O beautiful for spacious skies,
for amber waves of grain,
For purple mountain majesties,
above the fruited plain!
America! America!
God shed His grace on thee,
And crown thy good with brotherhood,
from sea to shining sea.

—Katharine Lee Bates

*Katharine Lee Bates wrote her poem America the Beautiful in 1893
after a visit to Pike's Peak, a 14,110-foot mountain in Colorado.
The music for this famous song is by Samuel Augustus Ward.*

UNIT TEST

A. CIVICS

Practice the questions and answers.*

1.	What ocean is on the West Coast of the United States?	The Pacific Ocean
2.	What ocean is on the East Coast of the United States?	The Atlantic Ocean
3.	What is the capital of the United States?	Washington, D.C.
4.	Name one state that borders Canada.	Maine Minnesota New Hampshire North Dakota Vermont Montana New York Idaho Pennsylvania Washington Ohio Alaska Michigan
5.	Name one state that borders Mexico.	California New Mexico Arizona Texas
6.	Name one of the two longest rivers in the United States.	The Missouri River The Mississippi River
7.	Where is the Statue of Liberty?	New York New York Harbor Liberty Island (New Jersey)** (Near New York City)** (On the Hudson River)** (** also acceptable answers)
8.	Name one U.S. territory.	Puerto Rico The U.S. Virgin Islands American Samoa The Northern Mariana Islands Guam

* Some questions have more than one possible answer. Only one answer is required unless the question asks for more.

B. CIVICS MATCHING

Match the question and the correct answer.

_____ 1. Name one state that borders Canada.

_____ 2. Name one state that borders Mexico.

_____ 3. Name one U.S. territory.

a. Puerto Rico

b. New York

c. Texas

C. KEY VOCABULARY

Write the correct word to complete the civics fact.

Alaska	California	Canada	Mexico	New York
	United States		Washington, D.C.	

1. The capital of the United States is _____.

2. _____ is north of the United States.

3. The country that borders Texas is _____.

4. One state that borders Canada is _____.

5. The Statue of Liberty is in _____.

6. Mexico is south of the _____.

7. The state that has the most people is _____.

D. READING AND WRITING

Say the question. Then listen and write the sentence you hear.

1. What country is north of the United States?

   _____
   CD 1: Track 29

2. What is the capital of the United States?

   _____
   CD 1: Track 30

3. What country is south of the United States?

   _____
   CD 1: Track 31

4. What is the largest state in the United States?

   _____
   CD 1: Track 32

5. What city in the United States has the most people?

   _____
   CD 1: Track 33

Civics Enrichment

Look at a local street map of your community. What kind of information do you see? Find your school on the map. Find where you and other students live. Look for other maps of your community (such as maps of bus routes or parks). Bring the maps to class. Discuss what kinds of information you see on the maps.

Make a big tourist map for visitors to your community! On your map, draw all the important places to visit and show where they are. Show all the important streets. Show any bus or train routes tourists can use to visit the places on your map.

Visit U.S. states and territories online! Go to: www.usa.gov/Citizen/Topics/Travel_ Tourism/State_Tourism.shtml—a website with links to all the states and territories. Click on a link and learn about a place. What are things to do there? What are the landmarks? How can you go there? Share your information with the class.

UNIT SUMMARY

KEY VOCABULARY

READING

capital
city
country
has
is
largest
most
north
of
people
south
the
United States
what

WRITING

Alaska
Canada
capital
has
is
largest
Mexico
most
New York City
north
of
people
south
the
United States
Washington, D.C.

GEOGRAPHY

Atlantic Ocean
Canada
capital
city
country
East Coast
Hudson River
island
Liberty Island
map
Mexico
Mississippi River
Missouri River
New York Harbor
ocean
Pacific Ocean
river
state
United States of America
West Coast

STATES

Alaska
Arizona
California
Idaho
Maine
Michigan
Minnesota
Missouri
Montana
New Hampshire
New Jersey
New Mexico
New York
North Dakota
Ohio
Pennsylvania
South Dakota
Texas
Vermont
Washington

CITIES

Hollywood
New York City
Philadelphia
St. Louis
San Antonio
San Francisco
Washington, D.C.

U.S. TERRITORIES

American Samoa
Guam
Northern Mariana
  Islands
Puerto Rico
U.S. Virgin Islands

COMPASS DIRECTIONS

east
north
south
west

GRAMMAR

TO BE
The United States **is** a large country.

WH-QUESTIONS
What is the capital of the U.S.?
Where is the Statue of Liberty?
Which states do you want to visit?
Why?

YES/NO QUESTIONS
Is the United States a large country?
Are you ready for some civics
  questions?

SHORT ANSWERS
Yes, it is.
No, it isn't.

FUNCTIONAL EXPRESSIONS

ASKING FOR REPETITION
I'm sorry. Please repeat the
  question.

CLARIFYING
I'm sorry. Did you say ____?

THE FLAG

- **There Is / There Are**
- **Singular / Plural**
- **Have / Has**
- **WH-Questions**

VOCABULARY PREVIEW

CD 1: Track 34

1. flag
2. flagpole
3. stars
4. stripes
5. Pledge of Allegiance

CD 1: Track 35

There are three colors on the flag of the United States.
The flag is red, white, and blue.

There are fifty states in the United States.
There are fifty stars on the American flag.
The flag has fifty stars because there is one star for
each state.
Each star represents a state.
The stars are white.

The American flag has thirteen stripes.
The stripes represent the original colonies.
The first thirteen states were called colonies.
There are thirteen stripes because there were thirteen
original colonies.
The stripes are red and white.

Check-Up

Vocabulary Check

1. The American flag is red, white, and _____<u>blue</u>_____.

2. There are thirteen _____ on the American flag.

3. There are fifty _____ on the American flag.

4. The stripes on the flag are _____ and white.

5. The first thirteen states were called _____.

> blue
>
> colonies
>
> red
>
> stars
>
> stripes

Grammar Check

1. _____<u>There are</u>_____ fifty stars on the American flag.

2. _____ one star for each state.

3. _____ fifty states in the United States.

4. _____ thirteen stripes on the flag.

5. _____ one stripe for each of the thirteen original colonies.

> There is
>
> There are

Civics Check

CD 1: Track 36

*Practice the questions and answers.**

1. Why does the flag have thirteen stripes?	Because there were thirteen original colonies. Because the stripes represent the original colonies.
2. Why does the flag have fifty stars?	Because there is one star for each state. Because there are fifty states. Because each star represents a state.

* Some questions have more than one possible answer. Only one answer is required unless the question asks for more.

Your Native Country's Flag

Draw and describe the flag of your native country. What are the colors of the flag? What's on it? Why? Share your drawing and information with other students.

I pledge allegiance
to the flag
of the United States of America,
and to the republic
for which it stands,
one nation,
under God,
indivisible,
with liberty
and justice
for all.

Astronauts Neil Armstrong and Buzz Aldrin plant the U.S. flag on the moon on July 20, 1969.

U.S. Marines raise the U.S. flag at the top of Mount Suribachi, a mountain on the island of Iwo Jima, during a World War II battle on February 23, 1945.

Firefighters raise the American flag at the site of the World Trade Center in New York City after the terrorist attack on September 11, 2001.

Practice with other students. Take turns asking and answering the questions. CD 1: Track 38

A. Why does the flag have fifty stars?

B. I'm sorry. Could you please repeat the question?

A. Yes. Why does the flag have fifty stars?

B. _____ *

A. That's correct.

> Because there is one star for each state.
>
> Because there are fifty states.
>
> Because each star represents a state.

A. Why does the flag have thirteen stripes?

B. I'm sorry. Could you please say that again?

A. Sure. Why does the flag have thirteen stripes?

B. _____ *

A. That's right.

> Because there were thirteen original colonies.
>
> Because the stripes represent the original colonies.

A. What do we show loyalty to when we say the Pledge of Allegiance?

B. I'm sorry. Could you please repeat that?

A. Certainly. When we say the Pledge of Allegiance, what do we show loyalty to?

B. _____ *

A. Very good.

> The United States.
>
> The flag.

* Some questions have more than one possible answer. Only one answer is required unless the question asks for more.

A. CIVICS

Practice the questions and answers.*

1. Why does the flag have thirteen stripes?	Because there were thirteen original colonies. Because the stripes represent the original colonies.
2. Why does the flag have fifty stars?	Because there is one star for each state. Because there are fifty states. Because each star represents a state.
3. What do we show loyalty to when we say the Pledge of Allegiance?	The United States. The flag.

* Some questions have more than one possible answer. Only one answer is required unless
  the question asks for more.

B. CIVICS MATCHING

Match the question and the correct answer.

_____ 1. Why does the flag have fifty stars?

    a. Because there were thirteen original colonies.

_____ 2. What are the colors on the American flag?

    b. Red, white, and blue.

_____ 3. Why does the flag have thirteen stripes?

    c. Because there are fifty states.

C. GRAMMAR

Choose the correct answer.

1. There   is   are   fifty states in the United States.

2. The American flag   has   have   fifty stars.

3. There   is   are   one star for each state.

4. The colors of the American flag   is   are   red, white, and blue.

5. The American flag   has   have   thirteen stripes.

6. The stripes   is   are   red and white.

7. There   is   are   thirteen stripes because there were thirteen original colonies.

D. KEY VOCABULARY

Write the correct word to complete the civics fact.

blue	fifty	flag	red	state	states	white

1. The American _____ has three colors.

2. There are fifty _____ in the United States.

3. The stripes on the flag are _____ and white.

4. The American flag is red, white, and _____.

5. The stars on the flag are _____.

6. Each star on the flag represents one _____.

7. There are _____ white stars on the flag.

E. READING AND WRITING

Say the question. Then listen and write the sentence you hear.

1. What are the colors on the American flag?

   _____
   CD 1: Track 39

2. How many states does the United States have?

   _____
   CD 1: Track 40

3. What state has the most people in the United States?

   _____
   CD 1: Track 41

4. What is Washington, D.C.?

   _____
   CD 1: Track 42

5. What is the largest state in the country?

   _____
   CD 1: Track 43

Civics Enrichment

CIVIC PARTICIPATION

Discuss: Where do you see the flag of the United States in your community? What other flags do you see? What's on the flag of your state? What are the colors of your state flag?

PROJECT

Bulletin Board "Flags of the World" Project: On a large piece of paper, draw a color picture of the flag of your native country. Write some sentences about the flag. As a class, make a bulletin board display of all the flags and information. (You can also put photographs and names of students next to their flags.)

INTERNET ACTIVITY

Go to www.google.com or another search engine on the Internet. Type the key words "American flag." Look for information to answer these questions: When does the flag fly at half-mast (in the middle of the flagpole, not at the top)? If you want to fly the flag at night, what must you do? When does the flag fly in front of the White House in Washington, D.C.?

UNIT SUMMARY

KEY VOCABULARY

READING	WRITING	THE FLAG	PLACES	OTHER WORDS
American flag	Alaska	American flag	island	because
are	and	flag	Iwo Jima	colonies
colors	blue	Pledge of Allegiance	moon	loyalty
country	California	star	Mount Suribachi	native country
does	capital	stripe	mountain	original
have/has	fifty (50)	U.S. flag	New York City	plant (v.)
how many	flag		United States	raise (v.)
in	has	**COLORS**	World Trade Center	represent
is	is	blue		show (v.)
largest	largest	red	**EVENTS**	site
most	most	white	battle	state
on	of		terrorist attack	top
people	people	**PEOPLE**	World War II	
state	red	astronaut		
the	state	firefighter	**NUMBERS**	
United States	the	U.S. Marines	one (1)	
Washington, D.C.	United States		thirteen (13)	
what	Washington, D.C.		fifty (50)	
	white			

GRAMMAR

THERE IS/THERE ARE

There is one star for each state.
There are fifty stars on the flag.

SINGULAR/PLURAL

There is one stripe.
There are thirteen stripes.

HAVE/HAS

How many stars does the flag **have**?
The flag **has** fifty stars.

WH-QUESTIONS

What are the colors of the flag?
How many stars are there?
Why does the flag have fifty stars?

FUNCTIONAL EXPRESSIONS

APOLOGIZING

I'm sorry.

ASKING FOR REPETITION

Could you please repeat the question?
Could you please say that again?
Could you please repeat that?

BRANCHES OF GOVERNMENT

- **Simple Present Tense**
- **Have / Has**
- **Can**
- **To Be**

VOCABULARY PREVIEW

CD 1: Track 44

| the legislative branch | the executive branch | the judicial branch |

1. the Capitol
2. the Congress

3. the White House
4. the President and the Vice President

5. the Supreme Court
6. the Supreme Court justices

CD 1: Track 45

The government of the United States has three parts.
These parts are called the three branches of government.

The names of the three branches of government are
    the legislative branch,
    the executive branch,
    and the judicial branch.

The Congress is the legislative branch.
The President is in charge of the executive branch.
The courts are in the judicial branch.

There is a separation of powers between the branches of
    government.
This is a system of checks and balances.
It stops one branch of government from becoming too powerful.

Vocabulary Check

balances	branches	executive	government
judicial	legislative	powers	

1. The _____government_____ of the United States has three parts.

2. There are three _____ of government in the United States.

3. The President is in the _____ branch of the government.

4. The Congress is the _____ branch.

5. The courts are in the _____ branch.

6. There is a separation of _____ between the branches of government.

7. A system of checks and _____ stops one branch of government from becoming too powerful.

Civics Check

*Practice the questions and answers.**

1. Name one branch or part of the government.	The legislative branch Legislative Congress	The executive branch Executive The President	The judicial branch Judicial The courts
2. What stops one branch of government from becoming too powerful?	Checks and balances Separation of powers		
3. Who is in charge of the executive branch?	The President		

* Some questions have more than one possible answer. Only one answer is required unless the question asks for more.

Discussion

Describe the government in your native country: Does the government have different parts, or branches? What are they called? Who works there? Who is in charge of the government? Where is the government located?

The legislative branch of the government is called
   the Congress.
Senators and representatives are in the Congress.
They make the laws of the United States.
They work in the Capitol.*
The Capitol is a building in Washington, D.C.

The President is in charge of the executive branch.
The Vice President also works in the executive branch.
They enforce the laws of the United States.
The President lives and works in the White House.
The White House is in Washington, D.C.

The Supreme Court justices work in the judicial branch.
They explain the laws of the United States.
They work in the Supreme Court.
The Supreme Court is in Washington, D.C.

* The Capitol = the U.S. Capitol, the United States Capitol

Matching I

__b__ 1. senators and representatives

____ 2. the President and the Vice President

____ 3. the Supreme Court justices

a. the judicial branch

b. the legislative branch

c. the executive branch

Matching II

____ 1. the executive branch

____ 2. the judicial branch

____ 3. the legislative branch

a. makes the laws

b. enforces the laws

c. explains the laws

Matching III

____ 1. the Supreme Court

____ 2. the White House

____ 3. the Capitol

a. the executive branch

b. the legislative branch

c. the judicial branch

Answer These Questions

1. Who makes the laws of the United States? _____

2. Who explains the laws of the United States? _____

3. Who enforces the laws of the United States? _____

Discussion

1. Describe how the government works in your native country: Who makes the laws? Who are the leaders? Who works in the judicial branch? Is there a court like the Supreme Court? What are the names and locations of the important government buildings? (If you have pictures of these buildings, share them with the class.)

2. Discuss some U.S. laws you know about.

Grammar Check

Circle the correct answer.

1. The President   live   (lives)   in the White House.

2. Senators   work   works   in the Capitol.

3. The Vice President   work   works   in the executive branch.

4. The Supreme Court justices   explain   explains   the laws.

5. The President   enforce   enforces   the laws.

6. The U.S. government   have   has   three branches.

Questions and Answers

Practice the different ways to ask these questions. Then write the answers.

1.　　　Which branch of the government makes the laws?⎫
　　Which branch of the government does the Congress work in?⎭

　　_____

2.　　　Which branch of the government explains the laws?⎫
　　Which branch of the government does the Supreme Court work in?⎭

　　_____

3.　　　Which branch of the government enforces the laws?⎫
　　Which branch of the government does the President work in?⎭

　　_____

Listening

Listen and circle the correct answer.

CD 1: Track 48

1.　White House　Capitol

2.　White House　Capitol

3.　Congress　Supreme Court

4.　Congress　Supreme Court

5.　senators　the President

6.　senators　the President

Practice with other students. Take turns asking and answering the questions.

A. Now I'm going to ask you some civics questions.

B. All right.

A. Name one branch of the government.

B. Could you please repeat the question?

A. Can you name one part of the government?

B. Yes. _____ *

A. Who is in charge of the executive branch?

B. The President.

A. And do you know what stops one branch of government from becoming too powerful?

B. I'm sorry. Could you say that one more time?

A. Something stops one branch of government from having more power than the other branches. Do you know what it is?

B. Yes. _____ *

The legislative branch.	The executive branch.	The judicial branch.
Legislative.	Executive.	Judicial.
Congress.	The President.	The courts.

Checks and balances.
Separation of powers.

* Some questions have more than one possible answer. Only one answer is required unless the question asks for more.

A. CIVICS

Practice the questions and answers.*

1. Name one branch or part of the government.	The legislative branch Legislative Congress The executive branch Executive The President The judicial branch Judicial The courts
2. What stops one branch of government from becoming too powerful?	Checks and balances Separation of powers
3. Who is in charge of the executive branch?	The President

* Some questions have more than one possible answer. Only one answer is required unless the question asks for more.

B. CIVICS MATCHING

Match the question and the correct answer.

_____ 1. Who works in the legislative branch?

_____ 2. Who works in the judicial branch?

_____ 3. Who works in the executive branch?

_____ 4. What stops one branch of government from becoming too powerful?

a. The Supreme Court justices

b. The President and Vice President

c. Checks and balances

d. Senators and representatives

C. GRAMMAR

Choose the correct answer.

1. The President   is   are   in charge of the executive branch.

2. Senators   work   works   in the Capitol.

3. The President   live   lives   in the White House.

4. The U.S. government   has   have   three branches.

D. KEY VOCABULARY

Write the correct word to complete the civics fact.

Congress	President	Senators	United States
Washington, D.C.		White House	

1. The _____ is in charge of the executive branch.

2. The _____ is the legislative branch of the government.

3. The Supreme Court is in _____.

4. The President lives in the _____.

5. _____ are in the Congress.

6. The Supreme Court explains the laws of the _____.

E. READING AND WRITING

Say the question. Then listen and write the sentence you hear.

1. Where does the Congress of the United States meet?

   _____

   CD 1: Track 50

2. Who lives in the White House?

   _____

   CD 1: Track 51

3. Where is the White House?

   _____

   CD 1: Track 52

4. Where do United States Senators meet?

   _____

   CD 1: Track 53

5. Where does the President live?

   _____

   CD 1: Track 54

Civics Enrichment

CIVIC PARTICIPATION

Field Trip Preparation: Prepare for a visit to the local office of your representative in the U.S. Congress. Practice conversations with other students so you are ready for the meeting: introduce yourselves, tell where you are from, tell about when and why you came to the United States, describe what you are learning in school, and tell about your plans for the future.

COMMUNITY ISSUES

Discuss with other students: What problems or issues are important to you? What do you want to talk about when you visit your representative? What opinions do you want to share?

INTERNET ACTIVITY

Visit your representative online! Go to www.house.gov/—the website of the U.S. House of Representatives. You can find your representative by name, by state, or by your zip code. Visit your representative's website. What kind of information does it have?

UNIT SUMMARY

KEY VOCABULARY

READING	WRITING	GOVERNMENT	PEOPLE	QUESTION WORDS
Congress	Congress	branches	Congress	what
do	in	courts	President	where
does	is	enforce the laws	representative	which
in	lives	executive	senator	who
is	meet/meets	explain the laws	Supreme Court justice	
lives	of	judicial	Vice President	**OTHER WORDS**
meet	President	laws		called
of	Senators	legislative	**BUILDINGS & PLACES**	can
President	the	make the laws	Capitol	have/has
Senators	United States	parts	Supreme Court	in charge of
the	Washington, D.C.	separation of powers	Washington, D.C.	live
United States	White House	system of checks and	White House	name (v.)
where		balances		powerful
White House				work
who				

GRAMMAR

SIMPLE PRESENT TENSE

They **work** in the Capitol.
The President **works** in the White House.

HAVE/HAS

The government **has** three branches.

CAN

Can you name one part of the government?

TO BE

The White House **is** in Washington, D.C.
Senators **are** in the Congress.

FUNCTIONAL EXPRESSIONS

APOLOGIZING

I'm sorry.

ASKING FOR REPETITION

Could you please repeat the question?
Could you say that one more time?

THE SENATE
THE HOUSE OF REPRESENTATIVES
THE PRESIDENT
THE PRESIDENT'S CABINET
THE SUPREME COURT

- **Simple Present Tense vs. To Be**
- **There Are**
- **Time Expressions**
- **Question Formation**

VOCABULARY PREVIEW

CD 1: Track 55

the legislative branch

1. the Senate
2. senator
3. the House of
   Representatives
4. representative

the executive branch

5. the President
6. the Vice President

the judicial branch

7. the Supreme Court
8. the Chief Justice of
   the United States

The Congress of the United States is the legislative branch of the
    government.
It is the national legislature.
The legislative branch makes the federal laws of the United States.
The Congress has two parts: the Senate and the House of
    Representatives.

U.S. senators work in the Senate.
There are one hundred U.S. senators.
There are two U.S. senators from each state.
A senator represents all the people of a state.
We elect a U.S. senator for six years.

Check-Up

Vocabulary Check

| laws | legislative | senators | six | two |

1. The Congress is the _____**legislative**_____ branch of the government.

2. There are one hundred _____ in the Senate.

3. We elect a U.S. senator for _____ years.

4. There are _____ U.S. senators from each state.

5. The Congress makes the federal _____ of the United States.

Civics Check

Practice the questions and answers. *

CD 1: Track 57

1. Who makes federal laws?	Congress The Senate and House The Senate and House of Representatives The U.S. legislature The national legislature
2. What are the two parts of the U.S. Congress?	The Senate and House The Senate and House of Representatives
3. How many U.S. senators are there?	One hundred (100)
4. We elect a U.S. senator for how many years?	Six (6)
5. Who does a U.S. senator represent?	All the people of the state
6. Who is one of your state's U.S. senators now?	_____

	(If you live in Washington, D.C., answer:
	    The District of Columbia doesn't have a U.S.
	    senator.
	If you live in a U.S. territory, answer:
	    We don't have a U.S. senator.)

* Some questions have more than one possible answer. Only one answer is required unless the question asks for more.

The House of Representatives

CD 1: Track 58

The Congress of the United States is the legislative branch of the government.
The legislative branch makes the federal laws of the United States.
The Congress has two parts: the Senate and the House of Representatives.

U.S. representatives work in the House of Representatives.
A representative is also called a *congressperson* (or *congressman* or *congresswoman*).
The House of Representatives has 435 voting members.

Some states have more representatives than other states.
This is because of the state's population.
Some states have more people.
States with more people have more representatives.
A representative represents the people in a Congressional district.
We elect a U.S. representative for two years.

Paul Ryan is the Speaker of the House of Representatives. He represents the First Congressional District of Wisconsin. As Speaker, he is the leader of the House of Representatives.

J Check-Up

Vocabulary Check

| Congress | district | House | representatives | two |

1. The _____Congress_____ is the legislative branch of the government.

2. There are 435 _____ in the Congress.

3. We elect a representative for _____ years.

4. A representative represents the people in a Congressional _____.

5. The _____ of Representatives has 435 voting members.

Civics Check

CD 1: Track 59

Practice the questions and answers.*

1.	The House of Representatives has how many voting members?	Four hundred thirty-five (435)
2.	We elect a U.S. representative for how many years?	Two (2)
3.	Why do some states have more representatives than other states?	Because of the state's population Because they have more people Because some states have more people
4.	What is the name of the Speaker of the House of Representatives now?	Paul Ryan
5.	Name your U.S. representative.	_____ (If you live in a U.S. territory, you can give the name of the territory's non-voting delegate or resident commissioner, or answer: We don't have a voting representative in Congress.)

* Some questions have more than one possible answer. Only one answer is required unless the question asks for more.

CD 1: Track 60

The President of the United States is the head of the executive
branch of the government.

The executive branch enforces the laws of the United States.

The President is the chief executive.

The President is the Commander-in-Chief of the military.

When the Congress wants to make a new law, it writes the law in a
document called a bill.

The Senate and the House of Representatives must pass the bill to
approve it.

Then the bill goes to the President.

If the President approves it, the President signs the bill and it
becomes a law.

If the President doesn't approve it, the President can veto the bill
and it doesn't become a law.

The President lives and works in the White House.
The American people elect a President for four years.
The President's term is four years.
The President can serve two terms.
We vote for President in November.

The Vice President works with the President.
The American people elect the President and the Vice President at the same time.
If the President can no longer serve, the Vice President becomes the President.
If both the President and the Vice President can no longer serve, the Speaker of the House of Representatives becomes the President.

The name of the President of the United States now is Donald Trump.*
The name of the Vice President of the United States now is Mike Pence.**

 * Donald J. Trump
** Michael R. Pence

Check-Up

Vocabulary Check

| elect | executive | military | serve | White House |

1. The President lives in the _____White House_____.

2. The American people _____ a President every four years.

3. The President is Commander-in-Chief of the _____.

4. The President can _____ two terms.

5. The President is the head of the _____ branch of the government.

Grammar Check

Circle the correct answer.

1. The President (is) are the Commander-in-Chief.

2. The President live lives in the White House.

3. We vote votes for President in November.

4. The President and the Vice President work works in the executive branch.

5. The President sign signs bills to become laws.

The Answer Is "The President!"

Practice these questions and write the answers.

1. Who is the chief executive of the United States? _____

2. Who is the Commander-in-Chief of the military? _____

3. Who lives in the White House? _____

4. Who signs bills to become laws? _____

What's the Number?

1. A U.S. senator's term is ___6___ years.

2. A representative's term is _____ years.

3. The President can serve _____ terms.

4. Americans elect a President for _____ years.

5. There are _____ United States senators.

6. There are _____ representatives in the Congress.

Civics Check

CD 1: Track 61

*Practice the questions and answers.**

1.	Who is the Commander-in-Chief of the military?	The President
2.	Who signs bills to become laws?	The President
3.	Who vetoes bills?	The President
4.	We elect a President for how many years?	Four (4)
5.	In what month do we vote for President?	November
6.	If the President can no longer serve, who becomes President?	The Vice President
7.	If both the President and the Vice President can no longer serve, who becomes President?	The Speaker of the House
8.	What is the name of the President of the United States now?	(Donald) Trump Donald J. Trump
9.	What is the name of the Vice President of the United States now?	(Mike) Pence Michael R. Pence

* Some questions have more than one possible answer. Only one answer is required unless the question asks for more.

The President's Cabinet

 The President's Cabinet advises the President.

Secretary of Agriculture

Secretary of Commerce

Secretary of Defense

Secretary of Education

Secretary of Energy

Secretary of Health and Human Services

Secretary of Homeland Security

Secretary of Housing and Urban Development

Secretary of the Interior

Secretary of Labor

Secretary of State

Secretary of Transportation

Secretary of the Treasury

Secretary of Veterans Affairs

The Attorney General

The Vice President

Civics Check

CD 1: Track 63

Practice the questions and answers.

1.	What does the President's Cabinet do?	It advises the President.	
2.	What are two Cabinet-level positions?*	Secretary of Agriculture Secretary of Commerce Secretary of Defense Secretary of Education Secretary of Energy Secretary of Health and Human Services Secretary of Homeland Security Secretary of Housing and Urban Development	Secretary of the Interior Secretary of Labor Secretary of State Secretary of Transportation Secretary of the Treasury Secretary of Veterans Affairs Attorney General Vice President

* Important: You must name *two* Cabinet-level positions when you answer this question.

The Supreme Court and other federal courts are the judicial branch of
the government.
The judicial branch explains the laws of the United States.

The Supreme Court is the highest court in the United States.
It reviews the laws.
It decides if a law goes against the Constitution.

There are nine justices on the Supreme Court.
They serve for life.
The American people don't elect the Supreme Court justices.
The President appoints them, and the Senate approves them.

The head of the Supreme Court is the Chief Justice of the
United States.
The name of the Chief Justice of the United States now is
John Roberts.*

* John G. Roberts, Jr.
(Jr. = Junior)

John G. Roberts, Jr.
*Chief Justice of the
United States*

J Check-Up

Fact Check

Circle the correct answer.

1. The judicial branch   makes   (explains)   the laws of the United States.

2. There are   nine   ten   justices on the Supreme Court.

3. The President   elects   appoints   the Supreme Court justices.

4. The Supreme Court justices serve for   two terms   life   .

5. The head of the Supreme Court is the   Chief Justice   President   .

Grammar Check

Write the question words.

1. _____What_____ is the highest court in the United States?

2. _____ justices are on the Supreme Court?

3. _____ is the Chief Justice of the United States now?

4. _____ do the Supreme Court justices serve?

5. _____ branch of the government explains the laws?

| How long |
| How many |
| What |
| Which |
| Who |

Now answer the questions.

Civics Check

CD 1: Track 65

*Practice the questions and answers.**

1. What does the judicial branch do?	It explains laws. It reviews laws. It decides if a law goes against the Constitution. It resolves disputes. It resolves disagreements.
2. What is the highest court in the United States?	The Supreme Court
3. How many justices are on the Supreme Court?	Nine (9)
4. Who is the Chief Justice of the United States now?	John Roberts John G. Roberts, Jr.** (** Jr. = Junior)

* Some questions have more than one possible answer. Only one answer is required unless
the question asks for more.

Questions and Answers

Practice the different ways to ask these questions.

> Who's the Chief Justice of the United States now?
> Name the Chief Justice of the United States now.
> What's the name of the Chief Justice of the United States now?
> Can you name the Chief Justice of the United States now?

Now answer these questions.

1. Who's the President of the United States now? _____

2. Name the Vice President of the United States now. _____

3. What's the name of your U.S. representative in Congress now? _____

4. Who is one of your state's U.S. senators now? _____

5. Can you name the Chief Justice of the United States now? _____

Information Exchange: *Branches of Government*

	Legislative Branch		Executive Branch	Judicial Branch
	Senators	**Representatives**	**President**	**Supreme Court Justices**
Number	100	435	1	9
Term	6 years	2 years	4 years	life
Place of Work	Senate	House of Representatives	White House	Supreme Court
Job	Make the laws		Enforce the laws	Explain the laws

Study the chart. Then practice with another student. Ask and answer questions based on the information.

Who works in the _____ branch of the government?

How many _____s are there?

We elect (a/the) _____ for how many years?

Where do/does _____ work?

What does a/the _____ do?

CD 1: Track 66

Practice with other students. Take turns asking and answering the questions.

A. What are the two parts of the U.S. Congress?

B. The Senate and the House of Representatives.

A. How many U.S. senators are there?

B. One hundred.

A. We elect a U.S. senator for how many years?

B. Excuse me. Could you please say that again?

A. For how many years do we elect a U.S. senator? What is a U.S. senator's term?

B. Six years.

A. Who is one of your state's U.S. senators now?

B. _____

A. And who represents your Congressional district in Washington?

B. Do you mean who is my U.S. representative?

A. Yes—in the House of Representatives.

B. _____

Write a Letter

Write a letter about a problem or issue. In your letter, tell who you are, describe the problem or issue, and give your opinion. Send the letter to your representative in Congress, to a senator from your state, or to the President. Their addresses are:

Rep. _____   Senator _____
U.S. House of Representatives   United States Senate
Washington, DC 20515   Washington, DC 20510

The President of the United States
The White House
1600 Pennsylvania Avenue NW
Washington, DC 20500

You can also write to the President online using the "Contact Us" form on the White House website. Go to: www.whitehouse.gov/contact

You're the Judge!

You and your classmates are the justices of the U.S. Supreme Court. Discuss an issue that the Supreme Court is currently considering. Make decisions about the issue and share your opinions with the other justices.

Meet with your Representative in Congress

Call your representative's local office. Visit the office, or invite your representative to visit your class. During the meeting, introduce yourself, tell where you are from, and describe when and why you came to the United States. Describe what you are learning in school, and tell about your plans for the future. Give your opinions about problems and issues that are important to you. Then ask the representative some questions about his or her job.

A. CIVICS

Practice the questions and answers.*

1.	Who makes federal laws?	Congress The Senate and House The Senate and House of Representatives The U.S. legislature The national legislature
2.	What are the two parts of the U.S. Congress?	The Senate and House The Senate and House of Representatives
3.	How many U.S. senators are there?	One hundred (100)
4.	We elect a U.S. senator for how many years?	Six (6)
5.	Who does a U.S. senator represent?	All the people of the state
6.	Who is one of your state's U.S. senators now?	_____ (If you live in Washington, D.C., answer: The District of Columbia doesn't have a U.S. senator. If you live in a U.S. territory, answer: We don't have a U.S. senator.)
7.	The House of Representatives has how many voting members?	Four hundred thirty-five (435)
8.	We elect a U.S. representative for how many years?	Two (2)
9.	Why do some states have more representatives than other states?	Because of the state's population Because they have more people Because some states have more people
10.	What is the name of the Speaker of the House of Representatives now?	Paul Ryan
11.	Name your U.S. representative.	_____ (If you live in a U.S. territory, you can give the name of the territory's non-voting delegate or resident commissioner, or answer: We don't have a voting representative in Congress.)
12.	Who is the Commander-in-Chief of the military?	The President
13.	Who signs bills to become laws?	The President

* Some questions have more than one possible answer. Only one answer is required unless the question asks for more.

14.	Who vetoes bills?	The President
15.	We elect a President for how many years?	Four (4)
16.	In what month do we vote for President?	November
17.	If the President can no longer serve, who becomes President?	The Vice President
18.	If both the President and the Vice President can no longer serve, who becomes President?	The Speaker of the House
19.	What is the name of the President of the United States now?	(Donald) Trump Donald J. Trump
20.	What is the name of the Vice President of the United States now?	(Mike) Pence Michael R. Pence
21.	What does the President's Cabinet do?	It advises the President.
22.	What are two Cabinet-level positions?	Secretary of Agriculture Secretary of Commerce Secretary of Defense Secretary of Education Secretary of Energy Secretary of Health and Human Services Secretary of Homeland Security Secretary of Housing and Urban Development Secretary of the Interior Secretary of Labor Secretary of State Secretary of Transportation Secretary of the Treasury Secretary of Veterans Affairs Attorney General Vice President
23.	What does the judicial branch do?	It explains laws. It reviews laws. It decides if a law goes against the Constitution. It resolves disputes. It resolves disagreements.
24.	What is the highest court in the United States?	The Supreme Court

25. How many justices are on the Supreme Court?	Nine (9)
26. Who is the Chief Justice of the United States now?	John Roberts John G. Roberts, Jr.** (** Jr. = Junior)

B. KEY VOCABULARY

Write the correct word to complete the civics fact.

Congress	President	Senators	States

1. The _____ signs bills and vetoes bills.

2. There are 100 United States _____.

3. The Senate and the House are the two parts of the U.S. _____.

4. _____ that have more people have more U.S. Representatives.

C. READING AND WRITING   CD 1: Tracks 67-71

Say the question. Then listen and write the sentence you hear.

1. Who can vote for the President of the United States?

   _____
   CD 1: Track 67

2. When do people in the United States vote for President?

   _____
   CD 1: Track 68

3. How many United States Senators does the Congress have?

   _____
   CD 1: Track 69

4. Who elects the United States Senators?

   _____
   CD 1: Track 70

5. When do citizens vote for the government of the United States?

   _____
   CD 1: Track 71

Civics Enrichment

CIVIC PARTICIPATION

Field Trip or Classroom Visitor: Visit the local office of your representative in the U.S. Congress, or invite your representative to visit your class. (See page 56 for suggestions about what to do during the meeting.)

INTERNET ACTIVITY

Online Field Trip to the U.S. Capitol: Go to www.visitthecapitol.gov—the website of the U.S. Capitol Visitor Center. Click on "About Congress" to learn about what Congress does. Then click on "About the Capitol" to learn about the Capitol Building. Share what you learn with the class.

INTERNET ACTIVITY

Visit the White House online! Go to www.whitehouse.gov—the website of the President. Click on "The Administration" and then click on the links to learn about the President, the Vice President, and the Cabinet. Share what you learn with the class.

UNIT SUMMARY

KEY VOCABULARY

READING	WRITING	PEOPLE	GOVERNMENT	ACTIONS
can	can	chief executive	bill	advise
citizens	citizens	Chief Justice of the	Congressional district	appoint
Congress	Congress	United States	document	approve
do/does	elect	Commander-in-Chief	executive branch	become
elects	fifty (50)	Congress	federal courts	elect
for	for	congressman	government	enforce the laws
government	has	congressperson	House of	explain the laws
have	in	congresswoman	Representatives	go
how many	November	people	judicial branch	go against
in	of	President	law	live
of	one hundred (100)	President's Cabinet	legislative branch	make the federal
people	people	representative	legislature	laws
President	President	senator	military	pass
Senators	Senators	Speaker of the House	national legislature	represent
the	states	of Representatives	Senate	resolve
United States	the	Supreme Court	Supreme Court	review
United States Senators	United States	justices	U.S. legislature	serve
vote	vote	Vice President	White House	sign
when		voting member		veto
who				vote
				work

GRAMMAR

SIMPLE PRESENT TENSE VS. TO BE

The President **lives** in the White House.
The President **is** the chief executive.

THERE ARE

There are one hundred senators.

TIME EXPRESSIONS

The President's term is **four years**.
We elect a senator **for six years**.
We elect a President for **how many years**?
In what month do we vote for President?

FUNCTIONAL EXPRESSIONS

ASKING FOR REPETITION

Excuse me. Could you please say that again?

CLARIFYING

Do you mean . . . ?

TYPE OF GOVERNMENT & ECONOMY
THE RULE OF LAW
FEDERAL & STATE GOVERNMENT
PUBLIC OFFICIALS
THE CONSTITUTION
THE BILL OF RIGHTS

- **REVIEW: Simple Present Tense**
  - **To Be • Have / Has • Can**
  - **Must • WH-Questions**

VOCABULARY PREVIEW

CD 1: Track 72

1. vote
2. voting machine

3. federal government
4. state government

5. President
6. Governor

CD 1: Track 73

The United States is a republic.　→　*A STATE WHERE the SUPREME POWER is held by the people + their ELECTED REPRESENTATIVES with AN ELECTED PRESIDENT*
It has a democratic form of government.
It has a representative form of government.
The American people vote for public officials.
They elect the President, the Vice President, the senators, and the representatives.
These officials serve the American people.　　*Rather than a MONARCH*

A basic principle of American democracy is the *rule of law*.
Everyone must follow the law.
Leaders must obey the law.
Government must obey the law.
No one is above the law.

The economic system in the United States is a *capitalist economy*.
The producers of most goods and services are privately owned.
The government doesn't control them.
The economic system is also a *market economy*.
The market itself decides the prices of goods and services, not the government.

The New York Stock Exchange, New York City

Check-Up

Vocabulary Check

| capitalist | democratic | law | rule | vote |

1. The United States has a _____democratic_____ form of government.

2. The American people _____ for public officials.

3. No one is above the _____ in the United States.

4. The United States has a _____ economy.

5. A basic principle of American democracy is the _____ of law.

Grammar Check

1. The United States   does (has) a democratic form of government.

2. The American people   elect   elects   the President.

3. The United States   has   is   a republic.

4. No one   is   are   above the law in the United States.

5. U.S. government officials   serve   serves   the American people.

Civics Check

*Practice the questions and answers.**

CD 1: Track 74

| 1. What is the economic system in the United States? | A capitalist economy
A market economy |
| 2. What is the "rule of law"? | Everyone must follow the law.
Leaders must obey the law.
Government must obey the law.
No one is above the law. |

* Some questions have more than one possible answer. Only one answer is required unless the question asks for more.

Discussion

What form of government is there in your native country?
Do the people elect officials? Which officials?

What is the economic system in your native country?
Who produces goods and services? Who decides the prices?

Federal and State Government

Under our Constitution, some powers belong to the federal government:

> The power to print money
> The power to declare war
> The power to create an army
> The power to make treaties

Under our Constitution, some powers belong to the states:

> The power to provide schooling and education
> The power to provide protection (for example, police)
> The power to provide safety (for example, fire departments)
> The power to give a driver's license
> The power to approve zoning and land use

The Governor is the head of a state's government.

The name of our state is _____.

The Governor of our state now is _____.

The capital of our state is _____.

CD 1: Track 75

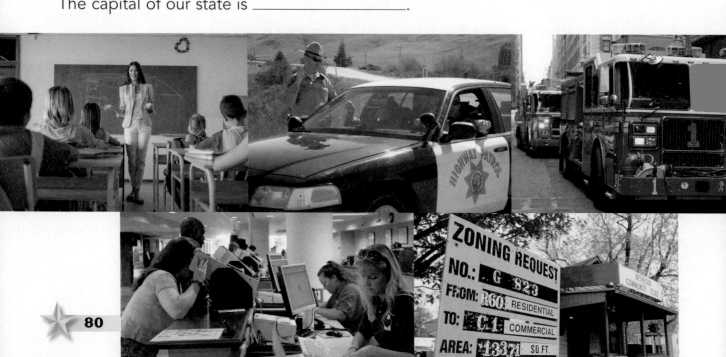

Vocabulary Check

government	governor	money	war	zoning

1. Some powers belong to the federal _____government_____.

2. The federal government has the power to declare _____.

3. State governments have the power to approve _____.

4. The head of a state's government is the _____.

5. The federal government has the power to print _____.

Federal or State Powers?

1. give a driver's license   federal (state)

2. declare war   federal   state

3. print money   federal   state

4. provide education   federal   state

5. provide fire protection   federal   state

6. make treaties   federal   state

Civics Check

*Practice the questions and answers.**

CD 1: Track 76

1. Under our Constitution, some powers belong to the federal government. What is one power of the federal government?	To print money To create an army To declare war To make treaties	
2. Under our Constitution, some powers belong to the states. What is one power of the states?	To provide schooling and education To provide protection To provide police To provide safety To provide fire departments To give a driver's license To approve zoning and land use	
3. Who is the Governor of your state now?	_____ (If you live in a U.S. territory, name the Governor of your territory. If you live in Washington, D.C., answer: The District of Columbia doesn't have a Governor.)	
4. What is the capital of your state?	_____ (If you live in a U.S. territory, name the capital of your territory. If you live in Washington, D.C., answer: The District of Columbia isn't a state. It doesn't have a capital.)	

* Some questions have more than one possible answer. Only one answer is required unless the question asks for more.

CD 1: Track 77

We the People of the United States, in Order to form a more perfect Union, establish Justice, insure domestic Tranquility, provide for the common Defence, promote the general Welfare, and secure the Blessings of Liberty to ourselves and our Posterity, do ordain and establish this Constitution for the United States of America.

Article. I.

Section. 1. All legislative Powers herein granted shall be vested in a Congress of the United States, which shall consist of a Senate and House of Representatives.

Section. 2. The House of Representatives shall be composed of Members chosen every second Year by the People of the several States, and the Electors in each State shall have the Qualifications requisite for Electors of the most numerous Branch of the State Legislature.

No Person shall be a Representative who shall not have attained to the Age of twenty five Years, and been seven Years a Citizen of the United States, and who shall not, when elected, be an Inhabitant of that State in which he shall be chosen.

Representatives and direct Taxes shall be apportioned among the several States which may be included within this Union, according to their respective Numbers, which shall be determined by adding to the whole Number of free Persons, including those bound to Service for a Term of Years, and excluding Indians not taxed, three fifths of all other Persons. The actual Enumeration shall be made within three Years after the first Meeting of the Congress of the United States, and within every subsequent Term of ten Years, in such Manner as they shall by Law direct. The Number of Representatives shall not exceed one for every thirty Thousand, but each State shall have at Least one Representative; and until such enumeration shall be made, the State of New Hampshire shall be entitled to chuse three, Massachusetts eight, Rhode Island and Providence Plantations one, Connecticut five, New York six, New Jersey four, Pennsylvania eight, Delaware one, Maryland six, Virginia ten, North Carolina five, South Carolina five, and Georgia three.

When vacancies happen in the Representation from any State, the Executive Authority thereof shall issue Writs of Election to fill such Vacancies.

The House of Representatives shall chuse their Speaker and other Officers; and shall have the sole Power of Impeachment.

Section. 3. The Senate of the United States shall be composed of two Senators from each State, chosen by the Legislature thereof for six Years; and each Senator shall have one Vote.

Immediately after they shall be assembled in Consequence of the first Election, they shall be divided as equally as may be into three Classes. The Seats of the Senators of the first Class shall be vacated at the Expiration of the second Year, of the second Class at the Expiration of the fourth Year, and of the third Class at the Expiration of the sixth Year, so that one third may be chosen every second Year; and if Vacancies happen by Resignation, or otherwise, during the Recess of the Legislature of any State, the Executive thereof may make temporary Appointments until the next Meeting of the Legislature, which shall then fill such Vacancies.

No Person shall be a Senator who shall not have attained to the Age of thirty Years, and been nine Years a Citizen of the United States, and who shall not, when elected, be an Inhabitant of that State for which he shall be chosen.

The Vice President of the United States shall be President of the Senate, but shall have no Vote, unless they be equally divided.

The Senate shall chuse their other Officers, and also a President pro tempore, in the Absence of the Vice President, or when he shall exercise the Office of President of the United States.

The Senate shall have the sole Power to try all Impeachments. When sitting for that Purpose, they shall be on Oath or Affirmation. When the President of the United States is tried, the Chief Justice shall preside: And no Person shall be convicted without the Concurrence of two thirds of the Members present.

Judgment in Cases of Impeachment shall not extend further than to removal from Office, and disqualification to hold and enjoy any Office of honor, Trust or Profit under the United States: but the Party convicted shall nevertheless be liable and subject to Indictment, Trial, Judgment and Punishment, according to Law.

Section. 4. The Times, Places and Manner of holding Elections for Senators and Representatives, shall be prescribed in each State by the Legislature thereof; but the Congress may at any time by Law make or alter such Regulations, except as to the Places of chusing Senators.

The Congress shall assemble at least once in every Year, and such Meeting shall be on the first Monday in December, unless they shall by Law appoint a different Day.

Section. 5. Each House shall be the Judge of the Elections, Returns and Qualifications of its own Members, and a Majority of each shall constitute a Quorum to do Business; but a smaller Number may adjourn from day to day, and may be authorized to compel the Attendance of absent Members, in such Manner, and under such Penalties as each House may provide.

Each House may determine the Rules of its Proceedings, punish its Members for disorderly Behaviour, and, with the Concurrence of two thirds, expel a Member.

Each House shall keep a Journal of its Proceedings, and from time to time publish the same, excepting such Parts as may in their Judgment require Secrecy; and the Yeas and Nays of the Members of either House on any question shall, at the Desire of one fifth of those Present, be entered on the Journal.

Neither House, during the Session of Congress, shall, without the Consent of the other, adjourn for more than three days, nor to any other Place than that in which the two Houses shall be sitting.

Section. 6. The Senators and Representatives shall receive a Compensation for their Services, to be ascertained by Law, and paid out of the Treasury of the United States. They shall in all Cases, except Treason, Felony and Breach of the Peace, be privileged from Arrest during their Attendance at the Session of their respective Houses, and in going to and returning from the same; and for any Speech or Debate in either House, they shall not be questioned in any other Place.

No Senator or Representative shall, during the Time for which he was elected, be appointed to any civil Office under the Authority of the United States, which shall have been created, or the Emoluments whereof shall have been encreased during such time; and no Person holding any Office under the United States, shall be a Member of either House during his Continuance in Office.

Section. 7. All Bills for raising Revenue shall originate in the House of Representatives; but the Senate may propose or concur with Amendments as on other Bills.

Every Bill which shall have passed the House of Representatives and the Senate, shall, before it become a Law, be presented to the President of the

The Constitution is the supreme law of the land.
It is the highest law in the United States.

The Constitution sets up the government.
It defines the rules for the three branches of government.
It says what each branch can do and what each branch cannot do.
It tells the Senate and the House of Representatives how to make laws.
It tells the President and the Vice President how to enforce the laws.
It helps the Supreme Court and other courts explain the laws.
It says that states can make their own laws.

The Constitution also protects the basic rights of Americans.

CD 1: Track 78

The people of the United States can change the Constitution.
A change to the Constitution is an amendment.
An amendment is an addition to the Constitution.
The Constitution has 27 amendments.

We call the first ten amendments the Bill of Rights.
The Bill of Rights gives rights and freedoms to all people in the United States.

The First Amendment gives Americans many important rights and freedoms.
It guarantees freedom of speech.
(Americans can say what they want to.)
It guarantees freedom of the press. _
(Americans can write what they want to.)
It guarantees freedom of religion.
(Americans can worship as they want to.
    They can practice any religion, or not practice a religion.)
It guarantees freedom of assembly.
(Americans can meet together as they want to.)
It guarantees the right to petition the government.
(Americans can ask the government to do something, or not do something,
    by giving the government a signed document called a petition.)

Check-Up

"Mirror" Questions

Practice these questions. Notice that they ask about the same thing.

What is the highest law in the United States? The Constitution.	What is the Constitution? The highest law in the United States.

Answer these "mirror" questions on a separate sheet of paper. Then practice asking and answering these questions with other students.

1. What is the supreme law of the land?
2. What is the Constitution of the United States?

3. What is an amendment?
4. What do we call a change to the Constitution?

5. What do we call the first ten amendments to the Constitution?
6. What is the Bill of Rights?

First Amendment Rights

Write the First Amendment right under the correct picture.

freedom of assembly freedom of religion	freedom of speech freedom of the press	the right to petition the government

1. _____

2. _____

3. _____

4. _____

5. _____

First Amendment Matching

<u>b</u> 1. freedom of the press

_____ 2. freedom of religion

_____ 3. freedom of assembly

_____ 4. freedom of speech

_____ 5. the right to petition

a. Americans can meet together as they want to.

b. Americans can write what they want to.

c. Americans can say what they want to.

d. Americans can ask the government to do something.

e. Americans can worship as they want to.

Civics Check

CD 2: Track 1

*Practice the questions and answers.**

1. What is the supreme law of the land?	The Constitution
2. What does the Constitution do?	It sets up the government. It defines the government. It protects basic rights of Americans.
3. What is an amendment?	A change to the Constitution An addition to the Constitution
4. What do we call the first ten amendments to the Constitution?	The Bill of Rights
5. What is one right or freedom from the First Amendment?	Freedom of speech Freedom of religion Freedom of assembly Freedom of the press The right to petition the government
6. How many amendments does the Constitution have?	Twenty-seven (27)
7. What is freedom of religion?	You can practice any religion, or not practice a religion.

* Some questions have more than one possible answer. Only one answer is required unless the question asks for more.

Discussion and Debate

1. In your opinion, do all people in the United States have equal rights and freedoms guaranteed in the Bill of Rights?
2. In your opinion, should there ever be limits on freedom of speech or other rights? Why, or why not? Give examples.

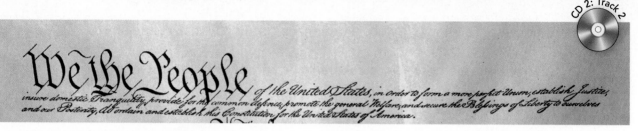

The idea of self-government is in the first three words of the Constitution. These words are *We the People*.

These three words describe the power of the people in the government of the United States.
The people give power to the government.
The government serves the people.

The introduction to the Constitution is called the Preamble.
The Preamble begins with these three famous words: *We the People*.

We the People of the United States,
in order to form a more perfect Union,
establish justice,
insure domestic tranquility,
provide for the common defense,
promote the general welfare,
and secure the blessing of liberty
to ourselves and our posterity,
do ordain and establish
this Constitution for the United States of America.*

Civics Check

Practice the question and answer.

The idea of self-government is in the first three words of the Constitution. What are these words?	We the People

* The entire Preamble is for enrichment and speaking practice. It is not required for the citizenship exam.

Practice with other students. Take turns asking and answering the questions.

A. Can you tell me the first three words of the Preamble?

B. The Preamble? Do you mean the first three words of the Constitution?

A. Yes.

B. We the People.

A. And what does the Constitution do?

B. _____*

> It sets up the government.
>
> It defines the government.
>
> It protects basic rights of Americans.

A. Do you know how many amendments the Constitution has?

B. Yes. Twenty-seven.

A. And what are the first ten amendments called?

B. The Bill of Rights.

A. Can you tell me one right or freedom from the First Amendment?

B. _____*

> Freedom of speech.
>
> Freedom of religion.
>
> Freedom of assembly.
>
> Freedom of the press.
>
> The right to petition the government.

A. What is the rule of law?

B. I'm sorry. Did you say "the supreme law"?

A. No. The rule of law. What is the rule of law?

B. I understand.

_____*

> Everyone must follow the law.
>
> Leaders must obey the law.
>
> Government must obey the law.
>
> No one is above the law.

* Some questions have more than one possible answer. Only one answer is required unless the question asks for more.

A. CIVICS

Practice the questions and answers.[*]

1. What is the economic system in the United States?	A capitalist economy A market economy
2. What is the "rule of law"?	Everyone must follow the law. Leaders must obey the law. Government must obey the law. No one is above the law.
3. Under our Constitution, some powers belong to the federal government. What is one power of the federal government?	To print money To declare war To create an army To make treaties
4. Under our Constitution, some powers belong to the states. What is one power of the states?	To provide schooling and education To provide protection To provide police To provide safety To provide fire departments To give a driver's license To approve zoning and land use
5. Who is the Governor of your state now?	_____ (If you live in a U.S. territory, name the Governor of your territory. If you live in Washington, D.C., answer: The District of Columbia doesn't have a Governor.)
6. What is the capital of your state?	_____ (If you live in a U.S. territory, name the capital of your territory. If you live in Washington, D.C., answer: The District of Columbia isn't a state. It doesn't have a capital.)
7. What is the supreme law of the land?	The Constitution
8. What does the Constitution do?	It sets up the government. It defines the government. It protects basic rights of Americans.

[*] Some questions have more than one possible answer. Only one answer is required unless the question asks for more.

9.	What is an amendment?	A change to the Constitution An addition to the Constitution
10.	What do we call the first ten amendments to the Constitution?	The Bill of Rights
11.	What is one right or freedom from the First Amendment?	Freedom of speech Freedom of religion Freedom of assembly Freedom of the press The right to petition the government
12.	How many amendments does the Constitution have?	Twenty-seven (27)
13.	What is freedom of religion?	You can practice any religion, or not practice a religion.
14.	The idea of self-government is in the first three words of the Constitution. What are these words?	We the People

B. READING AND WRITING

Say the question. Then listen and write the sentence you hear.

1. Who elects the President of the United States?

_____

CD 2: Track 5

2. Who votes for the Congress of the United States?

_____

CD 2: Track 6

3. When do people in the United States vote for the Congress?

_____

CD 2: Track 7

4. What is one right in the Bill of Rights?

_____

CD 2: Track 8

5. Where does the President of the United States live?

_____

CD 2: Track 9

Civics Enrichment

Field Trip: Visit your city hall or town government office. Meet with a local official. Take a tour of the building and learn about the services available in the different departments. Or visit your local government's website. What kind of information does it have?

"Class Election Day": Have an election in class. Run for class president or vice president. Give a campaign speech and tell students why they should vote for you. Or serve on the Board of Elections. Watch students vote. Count the ballots. Or be a TV news reporter! Interview the candidates and the voters, and report the election results.

Go to www.google.com or another search engine on the Internet. Type the key words "____ state government" (fill in the name of your state). Click on a link to your state's official website. What kinds of information do you see? Share what you learn with the class. (If you live in Washington, D.C., go to: www.dc.gov)

UNIT SUMMARY

KEY VOCABULARY

READING
Bill of Rights
Congress
do/does
elects
for
in
is
live
of
one
people
President
right
the
United States
vote/votes
what
when
where
who

WRITING
citizens
Congress
elect
for
freedom of
    speech
have
in
lives
November
of
people
President
the
United States
vote
we
White House

GOVERNMENT
branch
democratic
federal
form of government
House of
    Representatives
powers
representative
republic
self-government
Senate
state
Supreme Court

ECONOMIC SYSTEM
capitalist economy
goods
market economy
prices
services

PUBLIC OFFICIALS
Governor
leader
official
President
public official
representative
senator
Vice President

GOVERNMENT POWERS
army
driver's license
education
land use
money
police
protection
safety
schooling
treaties
zoning

THE CONSTITUTION & BILL OF RIGHTS
amendment
Bill of Rights
Constitution
First Amendment
freedom of assembly
freedom of religion
freedom of speech
freedom of the press
freedoms
law
meet together
petition
Preamble
rights
rules
say
supreme law of the
    land
worship
write

GRAMMAR

TO BE
The United States **is** a republic.
The first three words of the
    Constitution **are** We the People.

SIMPLE PRESENT TENSE
The people **vote** for officials.

HAVE/HAS
The Constitution **has** 27 amendments.

CAN
Americans **can** say what they want to.

MUST
Everyone **must** follow the law.

FUNCTIONAL EXPRESSIONS

CLARIFYING
Do you mean . . . ?
I'm sorry. Did you say ____?

INDICATING UNDERSTANDING
I understand.

NATIVE AMERICANS
CHRISTOPHER COLUMBUS
DISCOVERY
COLONIZATION

- Past Tense: Regular Verbs
- Past Tense: Irregular Verbs

VOCABULARY PREVIEW

CD 2: Track 10

1. Christopher Columbus
2. Native Americans
3. colonists
4. the *Mayflower*
5. Thanksgiving

Native Americans (American Indians) & Columbus

CD 2: Track 17

Christopher Columbus sailed from Spain in 1492.

He wanted to go to the Indies.

People in Europe liked things from the Indies.

Many Europeans traveled very far by land to get there.

Columbus hoped to find a better way to get there.

He wanted to sail there from Europe.

Columbus sailed west across the Atlantic Ocean.

He didn't land in the Indies.

He landed on some islands near the Atlantic Coast of
    North America.

Christopher Columbus
*Columbus Day is a
national holiday in
October.*

In stories and in school, children often learn that Columbus
    "discovered" America.

However, before the Europeans arrived in America, people already lived here.

Columbus called these native people Indians.

Today we call them Native Americans.

Columbus shipped hundreds of the Indians back to Spain to sell as slaves.

Most of them died on the way to Spain or soon after they arrived.

He ordered the Indians to find gold.

He punished or killed Indians who didn't find enough gold each year.

Hundreds of thousands of Indians died in the years after 1492.

Today there are 562 federally recognized tribal governments of American Indian tribes and Alaska Natives in the United States.

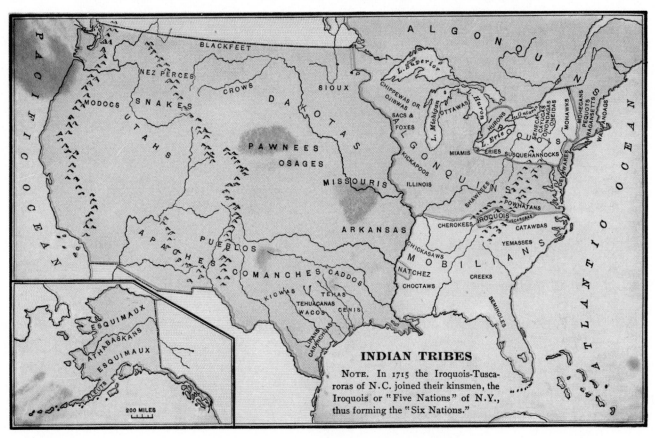

Map of the Indian Tribes of North America

Civics Check

CD 2: Track 12

*Practice the questions and answers.**

1.	Who lived in America before the Europeans arrived?	American Indians Native Americans
2.	Name one American Indian tribe in the United States.	Cherokee Apache Arawak Crow Navajo Iroquois Shawnee Teton Sioux Creek Mohegan Hopi Chippewa Blackfeet Huron Inuit Choctaw Seminole Oneida Pueblo Cheyenne Lakota (The tribes listed here are included in the official 100 civics questions and answers. Other answers are possible. There are 562 federally recognized tribal governments. USCIS Officers will have a list of these tribes. However, it might be best to name one of the tribes above.)

* Some questions have more than one possible answer. Only one answer is required unless the question asks for more.

J Check-Up

Vocabulary Check

Atlantic	Europeans	gold	Indians	islands	Spain	the Indies

1. Christopher Columbus sailed from _____.

2. He wanted to sail to _____.

3. He sailed across the _____ Ocean.

4. Columbus landed on some _____.

5. He called the people who lived there _____.

6. Native Americans lived in America before the _____ arrived.

7. Columbus ordered the Indians to find _____.

Grammar Check: *Regular Verbs*

Complete the sentences.

1. Columbus didn't *sail* to the Indies. He _____ to America.

2. Columbus didn't *want* to go to America. He _____ to go to the Indies.

3. The Indians didn't *live* in Europe. They _____ in America.

4. Columbus didn't *land* near the Pacific Coast. He _____ near the Atlantic Coast.

5. Columbus didn't *call* the native people Native Americans. He _____ them Indians.

6. Columbus didn't *order* the Europeans to find gold. He _____ the Indians to find gold.

Pronunciation Practice

CD 2: Track 13

Say these pairs of words. Practice the past tense endings.

[t]	**[d]**	**[ɪd]**
hope – hope**d**	sail – sail**ed**	want – want**ed**
like – like**d**	live – live**d**	land – land**ed**
punish – punish**ed**	die – die**d**	

Pronunciation Check

Say these words and write them in the correct columns. Then say the words in each column again to practice the past tense endings.

arrived	discovered	liked	hoped	landed	called
shipped	wanted	traveled	sailed	lived	punished

[t]	**[d]**	**[ɪd]**
	arrived	

Maps, Journeys, and Discoveries

1. Look at a map of the world. Trace Columbus's route from Spain to the New World. Then, trace your own route from your native country to the United States.

2. Write a story about your journey to the United States. In class, share your stories with each other. Then, publish them for other students in the school, your families, and your friends.

3. Imagine you are a Native American in the time of Columbus. Write a story about your life after Columbus lands on your island.

4. Tell about any explorers who came to your native country, and tell about the native people who lived there at that time.

The Colonies

People from England first came to America in the 1600s.
These people were called colonists.
The original thirteen states were called colonies.

The first colony was in Jamestown, Virginia.
Colonists from England came to Jamestown in 1607.
They came to America for economic opportunity.
They grew tobacco and traded with England.

In 1620 other colonists came to Plymouth, Massachusetts.
These colonists were called Pilgrims.
The Pilgrims came to America because they wanted
    the freedom to practice their religion.
They wanted religious freedom and political liberty.
They sailed to America on a ship called the *Mayflower*.

The Puritans also wanted religious freedom and political liberty.
They hoped to create a new church in America.
In 1629 the Puritans established the Massachusetts Bay Colony.

Roger Williams and his followers left the Massachusetts Bay
    Colony because of religious persecution.
The people there persecuted them for their religious beliefs.
In 1636 they went to Rhode Island.
They established Providence Plantation in Rhode Island.

Anne Hutchinson and her followers also left the Massachusetts Bay
    Colony because of religious persecution.
The people persecuted her because she spoke against the
    religious and political system.
She spoke against the persecution of Native Americans.
She also spoke about the rights of women.
In 1638 Hutchinson and her followers settled in Rhode Island.

J Check-Up

Vocabulary Check

| colonies | colonists | England | freedom | opportunity | persecution |

1. People from _____ came to America in the 1600s.

2. The original thirteen states were called _____.

3. The first _____ came to Jamestown, Virginia.

4. The colonists in Plymouth wanted religious _____.

5. The colonists in Jamestown wanted economic _____.

6. Roger Williams and his followers escaped religious _____.

Grammar & Pronunciation Check: *Regular Verbs*

Say these words and write them in the correct columns. Then say the words in each column again to practice the past tense endings.

| called | established | hoped | persecuted | settled | traded | wanted |

[t]	[d]	[ɪd]
_____	_____called_____	_____
_____	_____	_____
		_____

Now write these words to complete the sentences.

1. The Puritans _____hoped_____ to create a new church in America.

2. The Jamestown colonists _____ with England.

3. The Pilgrims _____ their ship the *Mayflower*.

4. The Pilgrims _____ religious freedom.

5. Colonists in the Massachusetts Bay Colony _____ Roger Williams and Anne Hutchinson.

6. Anne Hutchinson and her followers _____ in Rhode Island.

7. Roger Williams _____ Providence Plantation.

Grammar Check: *Irregular Verbs*

Study these irregular verbs.

> come – came
> go – went
> grow – grew
> leave – left
> speak – spoke

Now fill in the blanks with the correct words.

1. When did the first colonists from England come to Jamestown?

    They _____ to Jamestown in 1607.

2. What did the colonists grow in Jamestown?

    They _____ tobacco.

3. Why did Roger Williams and his followers leave the Massachusetts Bay Colony?

    They _____ because of religious persecution.

4. What did Anne Hutchinson speak against?

    She _____ against the religious and political system.

5. Where did Anne Hutchinson and her followers go?

    They _____ to Rhode Island.

Now practice the questions and answers with another student.

Civics Check

*Practice the question and answers.**

What is one reason colonists came to America?	Freedom Political liberty Religious freedom Economic opportunity To practice their religion To escape persecution

* Some questions have more than one possible answer. Only one answer is required unless the question asks for more.

Check-Up

Fact Check

Circle the correct answer.

1. The first colonists came to   Plymouth   Jamestown   .

2. The   Puritans   Pilgrims   sailed on a ship called the *Mayflower*.

3. The Puritans established a colony in   Massachusetts   Virginia   .

4. Anne Hutchinson spoke about the rights of women and
    Native Americans   Pilgrims   .

5. Anne Hutchinson and her followers settled in Rhode Island for
    religious freedom   economic opportunity   .

6. Roger Williams established   Plymouth   Providence   Plantation.

Listening

Listen and circle the correct answer.

CD 2: Track 16

1.
a. In Jamestown, Virginia.
b. In 1607.

2.
a. In Jamestown, Virginia.
b. In 1607.

3.
a. Because they wanted religious freedom.
b. In 1620.

4.
a. Because they wanted religious freedom.
b. In 1620.

5.
a. The *Mayflower*.
b. Plymouth.

6.
a. The *Mayflower*.
b. Plymouth.

Discussion

Some colonists came to America for religious freedom. Others came to America for economic opportunity or for other reasons. Discuss all the reasons people come to the United States today.

100

Your Immigration Story

Here are some common questions that people ask immigrants in the United States. Answer the questions in full sentences.

1. When did you come to the United States?

   _____

2. How did you travel to the United States?

   _____

3. Why did you come to the United States?

   _____

Information Exchange

Interview other students. Use these questions. Write the students' names and information below.

> What's your name?
> (Could you spell that, please?)
> When did you come to the United States?
> How did you travel to the United States?
> Why did you come to the United States?

	Name	When . . . ?	How . . . ?	Why . . . ?
1.				
2.				
3.				
4.				
5.				
6.				
7.				

Another Perspective

Look at the bottom picture on page 96. Imagine that you are the Native American on the left. Describe what you are thinking and feeling as the Pilgrims land in the place where you live.

CD 2: Track 17

Life was very difficult for the Pilgrims in the Plymouth colony.
Many of them died during the first year.

The Native Americans helped the Pilgrims.
They taught the Pilgrims how to grow corn and other food.
They taught them how to fish.
They also helped them build houses.

The Pilgrims wanted to give thanks for the many good things they had in America.
They celebrated a holiday in the fall of 1621.
They invited the Native Americans to a big dinner.
The Native Americans brought most of the food.

This holiday in the Plymouth colony is called the first Thanksgiving in America.
Actually, the Native Americans already had celebrations like this one.
Also, many people believe that the Jamestown colonists in Virginia celebrated the
    first Thanksgiving.
Others believe that colonists in the areas that are now North Carolina, Florida, or
    Texas celebrated the first holiday.

Americans still celebrate Thanksgiving.
Thanksgiving Day is on the fourth Thursday in November every year.
Families come together and have a big dinner.
They usually eat turkey, potatoes, corn, squash, and cranberries.
The Pilgrims and the Native Americans ate these foods at their celebration in 1621.

Check-Up

Vocabulary Check

| came | celebrated | helped | invited | taught |

1. The Native Americans _____ the Pilgrims in the Plymouth colony.

2. They _____ the Pilgrims how to grow food.

3. The Pilgrims _____ a holiday.

4. They _____ the Native Americans to a big dinner.

5. The Pilgrims _____ to Plymouth, Massachusetts, in 1620.

Grammar Check

Fill in the blanks with the correct words.

| come | came |

1. The Pilgrims _____ together to celebrate Thanksgiving in the Plymouth colony.

2. Every year American families _____ together to celebrate the Thanksgiving holiday.

| have | had |

3. Americans usually _____ a big dinner on Thanksgiving Day.

4. The colonists _____ a big Thanksgiving dinner in 1621.

| eat | ate |

5. The Pilgrims and the Native Americans _____ turkey at their Thanksgiving dinner.

6. Americans usually _____ corn and cranberries with their Thanksgiving turkey.

Discussion

1. What holidays did your family celebrate in your native country? How did you celebrate?

2. Do you celebrate Thanksgiving here in the United States? What do you do on that day?

3. Life was very difficult for the Pilgrims in the Plymouth colony. Was life difficult for you when you came to the United States? What didn't you know how to do when you came here? How did you learn?

Practice with other students. Practice the different ways you might hear the same question. Take turns asking and answering the questions.

CD 2: Track 18

A. Who lived in America before the Europeans arrived?

B. _____

A. Tell me who lived in America before the Europeans arrived.

B. _____

A. Can you tell me who lived in America before the Europeans arrived?

B. _____

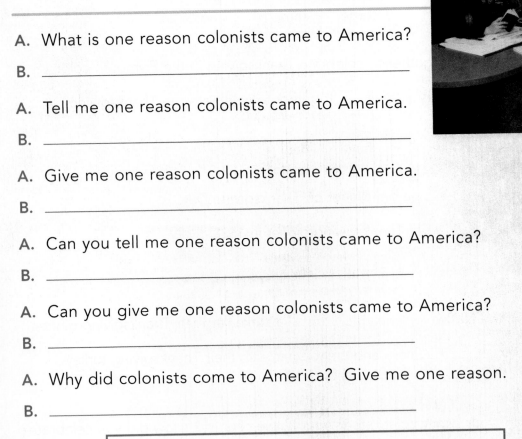

> American Indians.
>
> Native Americans.

A. What is one reason colonists came to America?

B. _____

A. Tell me one reason colonists came to America.

B. _____

A. Give me one reason colonists came to America.

B. _____

A. Can you tell me one reason colonists came to America?

B. _____

A. Can you give me one reason colonists came to America?

B. _____

A. Why did colonists come to America? Give me one reason.

B. _____

> Freedom.   Economic opportunity.
>
> Political liberty.   To practice their religion.
>
> Religious freedom.   To escape persecution.

CD 2: Tracks 19–20

My country 'tis of thee,
Sweet land of liberty,
Of thee I sing;
Land where my fathers died,
Land of the Pilgrim's pride;
From every mountainside,
Let freedom ring.

—Samuel Francis Smith

The Macy's Thanksgiving Day parade is a popular holiday tradition.

Plimoth Plantation in Massachusetts is a living history museum. It has a Pilgrim village and a Native American homesite. Nearby there is a re-creation of the Mayflower ship.

Jamestown Settlement in Virginia has a colonial fort, a Native American village, and re-creations of the three ships that brought settlers to the Jamestown colony in 1607.

A. CIVICS

Practice the questions and answers.*

1.	Who lived in America before the Europeans arrived?	American Indians Native Americans
2.	Name one American Indian tribe in the United States.	Cherokee Apache Arawak Lakota Navajo Iroquois Shawnee Crow Sioux Creek Mohegan Teton Chippewa Blackfeet Huron Hopi Choctaw Seminole Oneida Inuit Pueblo Cheyenne (The tribes listed here are included in the official 100 civics questions and answers. Other answers are possible. There are 562 federally recognized tribal governments. USCIS Officers will have a list of these tribes. However, it might be best to name one of the tribes above.)
3.	What is one reason colonists came to America?	Freedom Political liberty Religious freedom Economic opportunity To practice their religion To escape persecution

* Some questions have more than one possible answer. Only one answer is required unless the question asks for more.

B. GRAMMAR

Choose the correct answer.

1. American Indians   live   lived   in America before the Europeans arrived.

2. The Pilgrims   come   came   to Plymouth in 1620.

3. Every year on Thanksgiving American families   have   had   a big dinner.

4. The Pilgrims sailed to America because they   want   wanted   religious freedom.

5. Columbus didn't   want   wanted   to sail to America.

6. The first colony   is   was   in Jamestown, Virginia.

7. Roger Williams and Anne Hutchinson   go   went   to Rhode Island.

C. KEY VOCABULARY

Write the correct word to complete the civics fact.

American Indians	Columbus	free	October	November
	states	Thanksgiving		

1. The Pilgrims celebrated _____ in the fall of 1621.

2. The original thirteen _____ were called colonies.

3. Christopher _____ sailed from Spain.

4. _____ lived in America before the Europeans arrived.

5. Columbus Day is in _____.

6. The Pilgrims came to America because they wanted to be _____.

7. Americans celebrate Thanksgiving in _____.

D. READING AND WRITING

Say the question. Then listen and write the sentence you hear.

1. When is Columbus Day?

   _____

   CD 2: Track 21

2. Who lived in America first?

   _____

   CD 2: Track 22

3. When is Thanksgiving?

   _____

   CD 2: Track 23

4. Why do people come to America?

   _____

   CD 2: Track 24

5. When was the first Thanksgiving?

   _____

   CD 2: Track 25

Civics Enrichment

CIVIC PARTICIPATION

Field Trip: Visit a local supermarket. Which fruits and vegetables do you see in the produce section? What are the prices? Are there foods you like that the supermarket doesn't have? Tell the manager. Share your information with the class.

PROJECT

Celebrate Thanksgiving in your classroom! At home, cook a dish with Thanksgiving foods such as turkey, potatoes, corn, squash, or cranberries. Use a recipe from your native country, or use an American recipe. Bring the dish to school, and have a holiday meal. Share your recipe instructions with the class.

INTERNET ACTIVITY

Visit a colonial village online! Go to www.plimoth.org—the website of Plimoth Plantation in Massachusetts. Click on "Features & Exhibits" to learn about the village. You can also go to www.plimoth.org/education/olc/index_js2.html—a link to a multimedia program.

UNIT SUMMARY

KEY VOCABULARY

READING	WRITING	PEOPLE	PLACES	OTHER WORDS
America	American Indians	Alaska Natives	America	celebration
Columbus Day	be	American Indians	Atlantic Coast	church
	Columbus Day	children	Atlantic Ocean	colonial
come	first	colonists	colony	Columbus Day
do	free	Europeans	England	economic opportunity
first	here	family	Europe	freedom
in	in	Indians	homesite	gold
is	is	Native Americans	(the) Indies	holiday
lived	lived	native people	island	holiday tradition
people	November	Pilgrims	Jamestown Colony	*Mayflower*
Thanksgiving	October	Puritans	Jamestown, Virginia	national holiday
the	people	settler	Massachusetts Bay Colony	parade
to	Thanksgiving	slave	North America	political liberty
was	the	tribe	Plimoth Plantation	religious beliefs
when	to		Plymouth Colony	religious freedom
who	want	**FOOD**	Plymouth, Massachusetts	religious persecution
why	was	corn	Providence Plantation	rights
		cranberries	Rhode Island	ship
		potatoes	Spain	Thanksgiving (Day)
		squash	state	tobacco
		turkey	village	tribal government

GRAMMAR

PAST TENSE: REGULAR VERBS

[t]	[d]	[ɪd]
hop**ed**	sail**ed**	want**ed**
lik**ed**	liv**ed**	land**ed**
punish**ed**	di**ed**	invit**ed**

PAST TENSE: IRREGULAR VERBS

bring – brought	is/are – was/were
come – came	leave – left
eat – ate	grow – grew
go – went	speak – spoke
have – had	teach – taught

FUNCTIONAL EXPRESSIONS

WAYS TO ASK QUESTIONS

Who . . . ?
Tell me who . . . .
Can you tell me who . . . ?
What is one reason . . . ?
(Can you) tell me one reason . . . ?
(Can you) give me one reason . . . ?
Why . . . ? Give me one reason.

THE REVOLUTIONARY WAR
THE DECLARATION OF INDEPENDENCE

- **Past Tense: Regular Verbs**
- **Past Tense: Irregular Verbs**
- **Did / Didn't**

VOCABULARY PREVIEW

CD 2: Track 26

1. Boston Tea Party
2. George Washington
3. Declaration of Independence
4. Thomas Jefferson
5. parade
6. fireworks

CD 2: Track 27

Great Britain* wanted to control its colonies in America.

The colonists didn't want Great Britain to govern the colonies.

They wanted to have self-government.

They wanted to govern themselves.

The colonists paid very high taxes to Great Britain.

The colonists didn't have any representatives in Great Britain.

They called this *taxation without representation*.

The colonists didn't like British laws.

One law, the Quartering Act, required the colonists to provide quartering
(a room in their homes) and boarding (food) for the British army.

In 1773 Great Britain put a high tax on tea.

The colonists were very angry.

Some colonists in Boston, Massachusetts, went onto a ship that carried tea.

They threw the tea into the water in Boston Harbor.

This is called the Boston Tea Party.

The colonists met in Philadelphia in 1774.

They decided not to buy British goods.

They wrote to the King of Great Britain and complained about British laws.

At the meeting Patrick Henry said, "Give me liberty or give me death."

The colonists prepared to fight the British.

They prepared for war against Great Britain.

* In 1707 the separate kingdoms of England and Scotland merged and became Great Britain.

J Check-Up

Vocabulary Check

boarding	colonies	representatives	taxes	tea

1. Great Britain wanted to control its _____ in America.

2. The colonists didn't have any _____ in Great Britain.

3. The colonists paid _____ to Great Britain.

4. Some colonists in Massachusetts threw _____ into the water in Boston Harbor.

5. The Quartering Act required the colonists to provide quartering and _____ for the British army.

Boston Tea Party Grammar Check

Study the irregular verbs in the box. Then fill in the blanks with the correct words.

1. When did the British _____ a high tax on tea?

   They _____ a high tax on tea in 1773.

2. Where did some Massachusetts colonists _____ when Great Britain put a tax on tea?

   They _____ onto a ship in Boston Harbor.

3. What did those colonists _____ into the water?

   They _____ tea into the water.

> go – went
> put – put
> throw – threw

Now practice the questions and answers with another student.

Civics Check

CD 2: Track 28

*Practice the question and answers.**

Why did the colonists fight the British?	Because of high taxes Because of taxation without representation Because the British army stayed in their houses Because of boarding and quartering the British army Because they didn't have self-government

* Some questions have more than one possible answer. Only one answer is required unless the question asks for more.

The Revolutionary War

The Revolutionary War began in 1775.
It ended in 1783.
The American colonies fought Great Britain.

The colonies fought the war because they didn't like British taxes, they didn't
 like British laws, and they didn't have any representatives in Great Britain.
The colonists didn't want Great Britain to govern the colonies.
They wanted self-government.
They wanted to be independent from Great Britain.

The leader of the Colonial Army was George Washington.
The colonies won the war.

Grammar Check

Study the irregular verbs in the box. Then fill in the blanks with the correct words.

> begin – began
> fight – fought
> win – won

1. When did the Revolutionary War _____?

   It _____ in 1775.

2. What country did the American colonies _____ during the Revolutionary War?

   The colonies _____ Great Britain.

3. Did the Americans _____ the war?

   Yes, they did. They _____ the war in 1783.

Now practice the questions and answers with another student.

Did You Understand?

Answer these questions. Use full sentences.

1. What country did we fight during the Revolutionary War?

   _____

2. Why did the American colonies fight the war?

   _____

3. Who was the leader of the Colonial Army?

   _____

4. When did the Revolutionary War end?

   _____

Discussion

The colonists didn't like the taxes they had to pay to England. What do you pay taxes on? How does the government use this money?

The American colonists didn't want Great Britain to govern the colonies.
The colonists wanted to be independent.
They wanted to be independent of Great Britain.

The Revolutionary War began in 1775.
In 1776 the colonists met at Independence Hall in Philadelphia.
They decided to declare their independence from Great Britain.

Thomas Jefferson wrote the Declaration of Independence.
The Declaration of Independence said that the colonies were free from
    Great Britain.
It announced our independence from Great Britain.
Representatives of all thirteen colonies signed the Declaration of
    Independence.
The Declaration of Independence was adopted on July 4, 1776.

Grammar Check

Study the irregular verbs in the box. Then fill in the blanks with the correct words.

| begin – began |
| meet – met |
| say – said |
| write – wrote |

1. Where did the colonists _____ to declare their independence?

   They _____ at Independence Hall in Philadelphia.

2. When did Thomas Jefferson _____ the Declaration of Independence?

   Jefferson _____ the Declaration of Independence in 1776.

3. What did the Declaration of Independence _____?

   It _____ that the colonies were free and independent of Great Britain.

4. When did the Revolutionary War _____?

   It _____ in 1775.

Civics Check

CD 2: Track 31

Practice the questions and answers. *

1. What did the Declaration of Independence do?	It announced our independence from Great Britain. It declared our independence from Great Britain. It said that the United States is free from Great Britain.
2. Who wrote the Declaration of Independence?	(Thomas) Jefferson
3. When was the Declaration of Independence adopted?	July 4, 1776 (July fourth, seventeen seventy-six)

* Some questions have more than one possible answer. Only one answer is required unless the question asks for more.

Discussion

Is your native country independent?
Was there a revolutionary war in your native country? When?
Who did the people fight against?
Were there any famous revolutionary heroes?

The Declaration of Independence

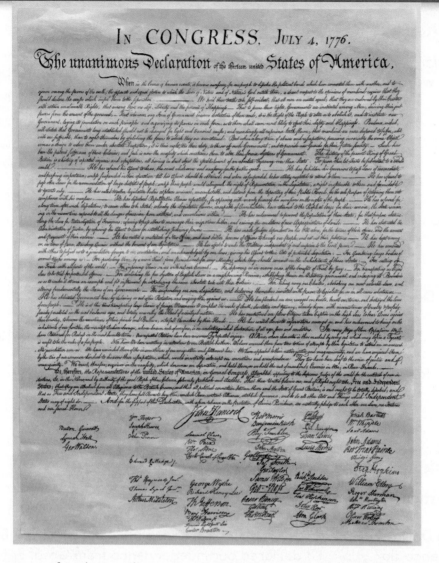

The Declaration of Independence is a very important document in American history.
It says that all people are created equal.
This is the basic belief of the Declaration of Independence.

It says that all people have rights that nobody can take away.
These rights are life, liberty, and the pursuit of happiness.

It says that the people tell their government what to do.
The government must do what the people say.
If the people want to, they can form a new government.

Based on these beliefs, the thirteen American colonies declared their independence.
The Declaration of Independence was adopted on July 4, 1776.

J Check-Up

Vocabulary Check

| document | equal | government | independence | liberty |

1. The Declaration of Independence is a very important _____.

2. The colonies declared their _____ on July 4, 1776.

3. The Declaration of Independence says that the people tell their _____ what to do.

4. The rights in the Declaration of Independence are life, _____, and the pursuit of happiness.

5. The basic belief of the Declaration of Independence is that all people are created

   _____.

Listening

CD 2: Track 33

Listen and circle the correct answer.

1.
   a. At Independence Hall in Philadelphia.
   b. On July 4, 1776.
   c. To be free and independent of Great Britain.

2.
   a. At Independence Hall in Philadelphia.
   b. On July 4, 1776.
   c. To be free and independent of Great Britain.

3.
   a. At Independence Hall in Philadelphia.
   b. On July 4, 1776.
   c. To be free and independent of Great Britain.

4.
   a. Great Britain.
   b. From 1775 to 1783.
   c. They wanted to be independent of Great Britain.

5.
   a. Great Britain.
   b. From 1775 to 1783.
   c. They wanted to be independent of Great Britain.

6.
   a. Great Britain.
   b. From 1775 to 1783.
   c. They wanted to be independent of Great Britain.

Civics Check

CD 2: Track 34

*Practice the question and answers.**

| What are two rights in the Declaration of Independence? | Life
Liberty
The pursuit of happiness |

* Important: You must give *two* rights when you answer this question.

Thomas Jefferson wrote the Declaration of Independence.

The thirteen colonies adopted the Declaration of Independence at Independence Hall in Philadelphia on July 4, 1776.

Jefferson's words are very beautiful.

This is the most famous part of the Declaration of Independence.

> We hold these truths to be self-evident,
> that all men are created equal,
> that they are endowed by their Creator
> with certain unalienable rights,
> that among these are life, liberty, and
> the pursuit of happiness.*

* For enrichment and speaking practice.
  Not required for the citizenship exam.

Civics Check

Practice the questions and answers.*

1.	Who wrote the Declaration of Independence?	(Thomas) Jefferson
2.	When was the Declaration of Independence adopted?	July 4, 1776 (July fourth, seventeen seventy-six)
3.	What are two rights in the Declaration of Independence?	Life Liberty The pursuit of happiness

* Important: When you answer question 3, you must give two rights.

Independence Day (The Fourth of July)

CD 2: Track 37

Every year on July 4th, Americans celebrate a national holiday.
The holiday is called Independence Day.
It is also called the Fourth of July.
On this day, Americans celebrate the birthday of the United States.
It's the country's birthday because on July 4, 1776, the thirteen colonies declared
   their independence.

Independence Day is a very happy celebration.
Many Americans get together with family and friends.
It is a summer holiday, and many Americans have picnics and barbecues outside.
In many cities and towns, there are parades and band concerts, and in the
   evening there are fireworks.

Civics Check

CD 2: Track 38

Practice the question and answer.

When do we celebrate Independence Day?	July 4 (July fourth)

Discussion

How do you celebrate Independence Day here in the United States?
Is there a celebration like Independence Day in your native country? When?
How do people celebrate the holiday?

119

Talking Time Line: Important Dates in U.S. History

Write these events on the correct lines in the time line below.

Colonists came to Jamestown, Virginia.
The Revolutionary War began.
Columbus sailed to America.
The colonies declared their independence.
Pilgrims came to the Plymouth Colony.
The Revolutionary War ended.

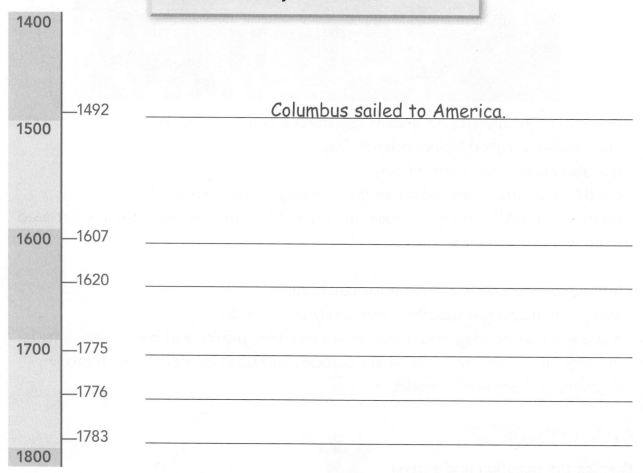

1400		
1500	—1492	Columbus sailed to America.
1600	—1607	
	—1620	
1700	—1775	
	—1776	
	—1783	
1800		

Now practice with another student. Ask and answer questions based on the time line.

When did _____?

What happened in _____?

Practice with other students. Take turns asking and answering the questions.
Practice what to do if you don't know the answer to a question.

A. What are two rights in the Declaration of Independence?

B. _____

A. And do you know what the Declaration of Independence did?

B. Yes. _____

A. Who wrote the Declaration of Independence?

B. Hmm. I studied that, but I don't remember.

A. He was the third President of the United States.

B. The third President? I'm afraid I don't know the answer.

A. It was Thomas Jefferson.

B. Oh, yes. Thomas Jefferson.

> Life and liberty.
> Liberty and the pursuit of happiness.
> Life and the pursuit of happiness.

> It announced our independence from Great Britain.
> It declared our independence from Great Britain.
> It said that the United States is free from Great Britain.

A. CIVICS

Practice the questions and answers.*

1.	Why did the colonists fight the British?	Because of high taxes Because of taxation without representation Because the British army stayed in their houses Because of boarding and quartering the British army Because they didn't have self-government
2.	What did the Declaration of Independence do?	It announced our independence from Great Britain. It declared our independence from Great Britain. It said that the United States is free from Great Britain.
3.	Who wrote the Declaration of Independence?	(Thomas) Jefferson
4.	When was the Declaration of Independence adopted?	July 4, 1776 (July fourth, seventeen seventy-six)
5.	What are two rights in the Declaration of Independence?*	Life Liberty The pursuit of happiness * Important: You must give *two* rights when you answer this question.
6.	When do we celebrate Independence Day?	July 4 (July fourth)

* Some questions have more than one possible answer. Only one answer is required unless the question asks for more.

B. CIVICS MATCHING

Match the question and the correct answer.

_____ 1. Who wrote the Declaration of Independence?

_____ 2. When was the Declaration of Independence adopted?

_____ 3. Who was the leader of the Colonial Army?

_____ 4. When do we celebrate Independence Day?

_____ 5. What rights are in the Declaration of Independence?

a. George Washington

b. Life, liberty, and the pursuit of happiness

c. July 4, 1776

d. Thomas Jefferson

e. Every year on July 4

C. KEY VOCABULARY

Write the correct word to complete the civics fact.

| free | Independence | Independence Day | July | rights | taxes | Washington |

1. The American colonists didn't like British _____.

2. George _____ was the leader of the Colonial Army.

3. Thomas Jefferson wrote the Declaration of _____.

4. The Declaration of Independence was adopted on _____ 4, 1776.

5. Life, liberty, and the pursuit of happiness are _____ in the Declaration of Independence.

6. The Declaration of Independence said that the colonies were _____ from Great Britain.

7. Our national holiday in July is _____.

D. READING AND WRITING

CD 2: Tracks 40-44

Say the question. Then listen and write the sentence you hear.

1. When is Independence Day?

_____

CD 2: Track 40

2. Who was the first President of the United States?

_____

CD 2: Track 41

3. What is the capital of the United States?

_____

CD 2: Track 42

4. Who was George Washington?

_____

CD 2: Track 43

5. What right do people in the United States have?

_____

CD 2: Track 44

CIVIC PARTICIPATION

What kinds of taxes do people pay to your local government? What does the local government do with this money? Get information from your city hall, town hall, or other government office. As a class, make a chart showing local government services and how much they cost.

PROJECT

Time Line Bulletin Board Project: As a class, make a large time line on a bulletin board. On the time line, show events that happened in the history of students' countries. Also show the events in U.S. history that you studied in this unit. Draw pictures of the events and write paragraphs about them.

INTERNET ACTIVITY

Go to www.ushistory.org/tour/index.html and visit historic Philadelphia online! Click on "Next Stop" to take a virtual tour, or click on these places in the Index: Betsy Ross House, First Bank of the United States, Independence Hall, Liberty Bell. What do you see? Why are these places important in U.S. history?

UNIT SUMMARY

KEY VOCABULARY

READING	WRITING	PEOPLE	EVENTS	ACTIONS	
capital	be	(the) British	band concert	adopt	govern
do	capital	colonist	barbecue	announce	have
first	first	family	Boston Tea Party	become	like
George Washington	free	friends	celebration	begin	meet
have	have	George Washington	fireworks	buy	merge
in	in	King	Fourth of July	carry	pay
Independence Day	Independence Day	leader	Independence Day	celebrate	prepare
is	is	Patrick Henry	(national) holiday	complain	put
of	July	representative	parade	control	require
people	of	Thomas Jefferson	picnic	create	say
President	people	writer	Revolutionary War	decide	sign
right	President			declare	take away
the	right	**PLACES**	**CONCEPTS**	end	tell
United States	the	America	equal	fight	throw
was	to	Boston	independence	form (v.)	want (to)
what	United States	Boston Harbor	liberty	get together	win
when	was	colony	life	give	write
who	Washington	country	pursuit of happiness	go	
	Washington, D.C.	Great Britain	rights		
		Independence Hall	self-government		
		Massachusetts	taxation without representation		
		Philadelphia			
		United States			

GRAMMAR

PAST TENSE: REGULAR VERBS

The colonists want**ed** to be independent.

DID/DIDN'T

What **did** the colonists do?
The colonists **didn't** like British laws.

PAST TENSE: IRREGULAR VERBS

become – became	pay – paid
begin – began	put – put
come – came	say – said
fight – fought	throw – threw
go – went	win – won
meet – met	write – wrote

FUNCTIONAL EXPRESSIONS

SAYING YOU DON'T KNOW

Hmm. I studied that, but I don't remember.
I'm afraid I don't know the answer.

THE CONSTITUTION
THE 13 ORIGINAL STATES
THE FEDERALIST PAPERS
BENJAMIN FRANKLIN
BRANCHES OF GOVERNMENT
THE BILL OF RIGHTS
GEORGE WASHINGTON

- Past Tense: Regular & Irregular Verbs
- Past Tense: Was/Were
- Present Tense Review

VOCABULARY PREVIEW

CD 2: Track 45

| 1. the Constitution | 3. freedom of speech | 5. freedom of religion |
| 2. the Bill of Rights | 4. freedom of the press | 6. freedom of assembly |

The colonies in America won the Revolutionary War in 1783.
They were free and independent states.
But they had a problem.
The thirteen states had thirteen separate governments.
There wasn't one strong national government.

Representatives from the states met in Philadelphia in 1787.
They met in a Constitutional Convention.
They wrote the Constitution.
These representatives are called the *Founding Fathers*.

The Constitution set up the government of the United States.
It established three branches of government: the legislative branch, the executive branch, and the judicial branch.
It defined the powers of the national government and the powers of the state governments.
It protected the basic rights of Americans.

The Constitution is the highest law in the United States.
It is the supreme law of the land.

Check-Up

Vocabulary Check

| branches | Constitution | Convention | government | powers |

1. The _____ is the supreme law of the land.

2. It set up the _____ of the United States.

3. It established three _____ of government.

4. It defined the _____ of the national and state governments.

5. It was written at the Constitutional _____ in Philadelphia.

Grammar Check

| was | wasn't | were | weren't |

1. After the Revolutionary War, the colonies _____ free and independent states.

2. They _____ colonies of Great Britain anymore.

3. There _____ a separate government in each state.

4. Before the Constitution, there _____ a strong national government.

Civics Check

Practice the questions and answers.*

1. What is the supreme law of the land?	The Constitution
2. What does the Constitution do?	It sets up the government. It defines the government. It protects basic rights of Americans.
3. What happened at the Constitutional Convention?	The Constitution was written. The Founding Fathers wrote the Constitution.
4. When was the Constitution written?	1787 (seventeen eighty-seven)

* Some questions have more than one possible answer. Only one answer is required unless the question asks for more.

Discussion

Describe your native country's constitution. How is it similar to the United States Constitution? How is it different?

The Thirteen Original States

The thirteen colonies became the thirteen original states.
These states were all on the Atlantic Coast.

CD 2: Track 48

The thirteen original states were
New Hampshire,
Massachusetts,
Rhode Island,
Connecticut,
New York,
New Jersey,
Pennsylvania,
Delaware,
Maryland,
Virginia,
North Carolina,
South Carolina, and
Georgia.

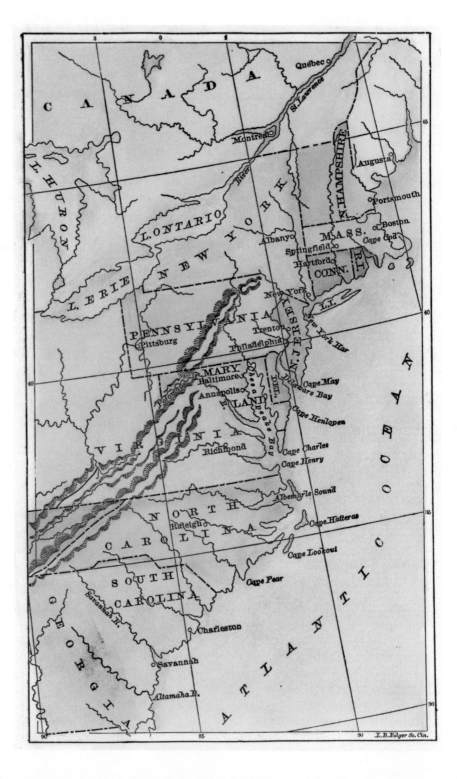

Practicing the Thirteen Original States

Write out the names of the original states in alphabetical order.

C o n n e c t i c u t

D _ _ _ _ _ _ _

G _ _ _ _ _ _

M _ _ _ _ _ _ _

M _ _ _ _ _ _ _ _ _ _ _ _

N _ _ H _ _ _ _ _ _ _ _

N _ _ J _ _ _ _ _

N _ _ Y _ _ _

N _ _ _ _ C _ _ _ _ _ _ _

P _ _ _ _ _ _ _ _ _ _ _

R _ _ _ _ I _ _ _ _ _

S _ _ _ _ C _ _ _ _ _ _ _

V _ _ _ _ _ _ _

Questions and Answers

Practice the different ways you might hear the same question.

There were thirteen original states. Name three.
There were thirteen original states. Please name three.
There were thirteen original states. Can you name three?
Name three of the thirteen original states.
Name three of the original thirteen states.
Please name three of the thirteen original states.
Can you name three of the thirteen original states?
Tell me the names of three of the thirteen original states.
Give me the names of three of the thirteen original states.
Can you tell me the names of three of the thirteen original states?

Now practice with other students. Take turns asking and answering the question.

Social Studies Enrichment

Prepare an oral report for the class about one of the thirteen original states.
Tell about the state today: its population, special geographical features,
important cities, products, and places to visit.

The *Federalist Papers*

CD 2: Track 49

After the Constitution was written in 1787, voters in the thirteen original states had to approve it.

In 1787 and 1788 newspapers in New York published 85 essays that supported the passage of the Constitution.

These essays were called the *Federalist Papers*.

They were written to convince voters in New York to vote for the new Constitution.

Alexander Hamilton, James Madison, and John Jay wrote the *Federalist Papers*.

But they didn't give their names as the writers of the essays.

The name of the writer on every one of the *Federalist Papers* is *Publius*.

THE

FEDERALIST:

A COLLECTION

OF *S. Chase*

E S S A Y S,

WRITTEN IN FAVOUR OF THE

NEW CONSTITUTION,

AS AGREED UPON BY THE FEDERAL CONVENTION, SEPTEMBER 17, 1787.

IN TWO VOLUMES.

VOL. I.

NEW-YORK:

PRINTED AND SOLD BY J. AND A. M'LEAN,
No. 41, HANOVER-SQUARE.
M,DCC,LXXXVIII.

Alexander Hamilton

James Madison

John Jay

Vocabulary Check

| approve | Convention | Papers | published | Publius | writers | written |

1. The Constitution was _____ in 1787.

2. It was written at the Constitutional _____.

3. The Federalist _____ supported the passage of the Constitution.

4. Voters in the thirteen original states had to _____ the Constitution.

5. James Madison was one of the _____ of the essays.

6. Newspapers in New York _____ the essays.

7. The name of the writer on every one of the Federalist Papers is

    _____.

Civics Check

*Practice the questions and answers.**

CD 2: Track 50

1.	What happened at the Constitutional Convention?	The Constitution was written. The Founding Fathers wrote the Constitution.
2.	When was the Constitution written?	1787 (seventeen eighty-seven)
3.	The Federalist Papers supported the passage of the U.S. Constitution. Name one of the writers.	James Madison Alexander Hamilton John Jay Publius
4.	What is the supreme law of the land?	The Constitution
5.	What does the Constitution do?	It sets up the government. It defines the government. It protects basic rights of Americans.

* Some questions have more than one possible answer. Only one answer is required unless the question asks for more.

PROFILE Benjamin Franklin

CD 2: Track 51

Benjamin Franklin was famous for many things.

He was a Founding Father.
He was the oldest member of the Constitutional Convention.

He was a U.S. diplomat.
He was the Ambassador to France from 1776 to 1785.

He was an inventor.
He invented the lightning rod, the Franklin stove, and bifocals (eyeglasses with two kinds of lenses to help people see near and far).

He was the first Postmaster General of the United States.
He figured out routes for delivering the mail.

He started the first free libraries in America.
For many years he was the writer of a popular yearly book called *Poor Richard's Almanack*.

Benjamin Franklin's cartoon supporting unity among the American colonies, 1754

Benjamin Franklin's yearly almanac, 1733

132

Vocabulary Check

Convention	diplomat	Father	libraries	Postmaster	stove	writer

1. Benjamin Franklin was a _____ in France from 1776 to 1785.

2. He was a "Founding _____."

3. He was the oldest member of the Constitutional _____.

4. He was the first _____ General of the United States.

5. He was the _____ of *Poor Richard's Almanack*.

6. He started the first free _____ in America.

7. He invented the Franklin _____.

Civics Check

CD 2: Track 52

*Practice the question and answers.**

What is one thing Benjamin Franklin is famous for?	He was a U.S. diplomat. He was the oldest member of the Constitutional Convention. He was the first Postmaster General of the United States. He was the writer of *Poor Richard's Almanack*. He started the first free libraries.

* Some questions have more than one possible answer. Only one answer is required unless the question asks for more.

Benjamin Franklin's Sayings**

Benjamin Franklin published many short and interesting sayings in Poor Richard's Almanack. These sayings were very popular. What do you think these sayings mean?

1. A penny saved is a penny earned.
2. Eat to live, and not live to eat.
3. Remember that time is money.
4. Well done is better than well said.
5. Early to bed and early to rise, makes a man healthy, wealthy, and wise.
6. The worst wheel of a cart makes the most noise.
7. The cat in gloves catches no mice.
8. When the well is dry, we know the worth of water.

** For enrichment. Not required for the citizenship test.

CD 2: Track 53

The Constitution established three branches of government: the legislative branch, the executive branch, and the judicial branch. The Constitution gave the rules for the three branches of government.

The legislative branch makes the federal laws of the United States.
The legislative branch is called the Congress of the United States.
The Congress has two parts: the Senate and the House of Representatives.
The Congress meets in the U.S. Capitol.

There are one hundred U.S. senators in the Senate.
There are two U.S. senators from each state.
A senator represents all the people of a state.
We elect a U.S. senator for six years.

The House of Representatives has 435 voting members.
Some states have more representatives than other states.
This is because of the state's population.
Some states have more people.
States with more people have more representatives.
We elect a U.S. representative for two years.

The Constitution gives many powers to the Congress.
One important power of Congress is the power to declare war.

The executive branch enforces the laws of the United States.

The President and the Vice President work in the executive branch.

The President is in charge of the executive branch.

The President is the chief executive of the United States.

The President is the Commander-in-Chief of the military.

The President signs bills to become laws.

The President also vetoes bills.

The President appoints members of the Cabinet.

The Cabinet advises the President.

A person must meet certain requirements to become President.

The President must be a natural-born citizen of the United States.

The President must be age 35 or older.

The President must live in the United States for at least 14 years before becoming President.

The President's term is four years.

The American people elect a President for four years.

The President can serve two terms.

We vote for President in November.

The President is inaugurated in January.

If the President can no longer serve, the Vice President becomes the President.

If both the President and the Vice President can no longer serve, the Speaker of the House of Representatives becomes the President.

The judicial branch explains the laws of the United States.

The Supreme Court and other federal courts are the judicial branch of the government.

The Supreme Court is the highest court in the United States.

There are nine justices on the Supreme Court.

The President appoints them, and the Senate approves them.

They serve for life.

Check-Up

Questions and Answers: *System of Government Review*

Practice with other students. Take turns asking and answering the questions.

1. Name one branch or part of the government.
2. Who is in charge of the executive branch?
3. Who makes federal laws?
4. What are the two parts of the U.S. Congress?
5. How many U.S. senators are there?
6. We elect a U.S. senator for how many years?
7. Who is one of your state's U.S. senators now?
8. The House of Representatives has how many voting members?
9. We elect a U.S. representative for how many years?
10. Name your U.S. representative.
11. Who does a U.S. senator represent?
12. Why do some states have more representatives than other states?
13. We elect a President for how many years?
14. In what month do we vote for President?
15. What is the name of the President of the United States now?
16. What is the name of the Vice President of the United States now?
17. If the President can no longer serve, who becomes President?
18. If both the President and the Vice President can no longer serve, who becomes President?
19. Who is the Commander-in-Chief of the military?
20. Who signs bills to become laws?
21. Who vetoes bills?
22. What does the President's Cabinet do?
23. What does the judicial branch do?
24. What is the highest court in the United States?
25. How many justices are on the Supreme Court?
26. Who is the Chief Justice of the United States now?

Now write the answers to the questions on a separate sheet of paper.

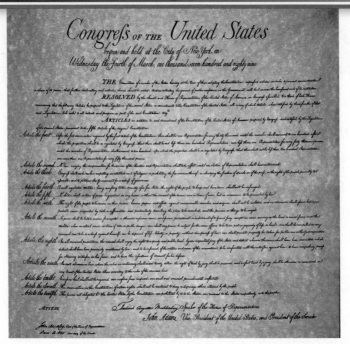

CD 2: Track 54

The people of the United States can change the Constitution.

A change to the Constitution is an amendment.

An amendment is an addition to the Constitution.

The Constitution has 27 amendments.

We call the first ten amendments the Bill of Rights.

These ten amendments were added to the Constitution in 1791.

The Bill of Rights protects the basic rights of Americans.

The rights of citizens and non-citizens are guaranteed by the Constitution and the Bill of Rights.

The First Amendment guarantees freedom of speech.

It guarantees freedom of the press.

It guarantees freedom of religion.

It guarantees freedom of assembly.

It guarantees the right to petition the government.

Other amendments in the Bill of Rights guarantee the rights of people who are accused of crimes.

They have the right to go to court, have a lawyer, and have a fair and quick trial.

The Bill of Rights also protects people in their homes.

The police need a special document from the courts before they can go into a person's home.

Matching

Match these First Amendment rights and their meanings.

_____ 1. Freedom of the press   a. Americans can say what they want to.

_____ 2. Freedom of assembly   b. Americans can worship as they want to.

_____ 3. Freedom of religion   c. Americans can write what they want to.

_____ 4. The right to petition   d. Americans can meet together as they want to.

_____ 5. Freedom of speech   e. Americans can ask the government to do something, or not do something.

Civics Check

*Practice the questions and answers.**

CD 2: Track 55

1. What does the Constitution do?	It sets up the government. It defines the government. It protects basic rights of Americans.
2. What is an amendment?	A change to the Constitution An addition to the Constitution
3. What do we call the first ten amendments to the Constitution?	The Bill of Rights
4. What is one right or freedom from the First Amendment?	Freedom of speech Freedom of religion Freedom of assembly Freedom of the press The right to petition the government
5. How many amendments does the Constitution have?	Twenty-seven (27)

* Some questions have more than one possible answer. Only one answer is required unless the question asks for more.

Discussion

1. How is the Bill of Rights important in our everyday lives? What can we do because of the freedoms guaranteed by the Bill of Rights?

2. Discuss examples from current events of rights and freedoms that are not allowed in some countries.

CD 2: Track 56

George Washington was the leader of the
  Colonial Army during the Revolutionary War.
He was an excellent leader.
The American people respected him very much.

In 1787 George Washington was the leader
  of the Constitutional Convention in
  Philadelphia.
At this meeting the representatives wrote the
  Constitution.

In 1789 George Washington became the first
  President of the United States.
He served two terms.

George Washington is one of the most
  important leaders in American history.
His picture is on the dollar bill.
Americans call George Washington the *Father of Our Country*.

Civics Check

CD 2: Track 57

Practice the questions and answers.

1. Who is the *Father of Our Country*?	George Washington
2. Who was the first President?	George Washington

CD 2: Track 58

What should you say when you need time to think about how to answer a question?
You can repeat one or two words in the question.
You can restate the question.
You can answer with a full sentence and put your answer at the end.
You can say an expression to fill time:

Let me see.	Let me think for a moment.	I studied this.
Let me think.	I know the answer.	

Practice with other students. Take turns asking and answering the questions. Practice what to say when you need time to think.

A. What is an amendment?

B. An amendment? Let me see. An amendment is _____.*

> a change to the Constitution
> an addition to the Constitution

A. What is one thing Benjamin Franklin is famous for?

B. Benjamin Franklin? Let me think. I know the answer.

_____*

> He was a U.S. diplomat.
> He was the oldest member of the Constitutional Convention.
> He was the first Postmaster General of the United States.
> He was the writer of *Poor Richard's Almanack*.
> He started the first free libraries.

A. The Federalist Papers supported the passage of the U.S. Constitution. Name one of the writers.

B. One of the writers of the Federalist Papers? I studied this. Let me think for a moment. One of the writers of the Federalist Papers was _____.*

> | | |
> |---|---|
> | James Madison | John Jay |
> | Alexander Hamilton | Publius |

* Some questions have more than one possible answer. Only one answer is required unless the question asks for more.

A. CIVICS

Practice the questions and answers.*

1.	What is the supreme law of the land?	The Constitution
2.	What does the Constitution do?	It sets up the government. It defines the government. It protects basic rights of Americans.
3.	What happened at the Constitutional Convention?	The Constitution was written. The Founding Fathers wrote the Constitution.
4.	When was the Constitution written?	1787 (seventeen eighty-seven)
5.	The Federalist Papers supported the passage of the U.S. Constitution. Name one of the writers.	James Madison John Jay Alexander Hamilton Publius
6.	There were thirteen original states. Name three.** ** Important: You must give *three* answers.	New Hampshire New Jersey Virginia Massachusetts Pennsylvania North Carolina Rhode Island Delaware South Carolina Connecticut Maryland Georgia New York
7.	What is one thing Benjamin Franklin is famous for?	He was a U.S. diplomat. He was the oldest member of the Constitutional Convention. He was the first Postmaster General of the United States. He was the writer of *Poor Richard's Almanack*. He started the first free libraries.
8.	What is an amendment?	A change to the Constitution An addition to the Constitution
9.	What do we call the first ten amendments to the Constitution?	The Bill of Rights
10.	What is one right or freedom from the First Amendment?	Freedom of speech Freedom of the press Freedom of religion The right to petition the Freedom of assembly government
11.	How many amendments does the Constitution have?	Twenty-seven (27)
12.	Who is the *Father of Our Country*?	George Washington
13.	Who was the first President?	George Washington

* Some questions have more than one possible answer. Only one answer is required unless the question asks for more.

142

B. KEY VOCABULARY

Write the correct word to complete the civics fact.

Delaware	dollar bill	Father of Our Country	freedom of speech
	New York City	President	Senators

1. George Washington was the first _____ of the United States.

2. George Washington is on the _____.

3. The first state that adopted the Constitution was _____.

4. There are 100 _____ in the U.S. Senate.

5. The First Amendment guarantees _____.

6. We call George Washington the _____.

7. Washington, D.C. wasn't the first capital of the United States. The first capital was

_____.

C. READING AND WRITING

Say the question. Then listen and write the sentence you hear.

1. Who was George Washington?

_____

CD 2: Track 59

2. Who is on the dollar bill?

_____

CD 2: Track 60

3. Why is George Washington the *Father of Our Country?*

_____

CD 2: Track 61

4. What was the first state in the United States?

_____

CD 2: Track 62

5. What city was the first capital of the United States?

_____

CD 2: Track 63

Civics Enrichment

CIVIC PARTICIPATION

As a class, discuss how people in your community exercise their rights guaranteed by the First Amendment. What are examples of freedom of speech, freedom of the press, freedom of religion, freedom of assembly, and the right to petition the government?

PROJECT

First Amendment Bulletin Board Project: As a class, make a bulletin board display about rights guaranteed by the First Amendment. Cut out newspaper headlines and photographs that are examples of these rights and display them on the bulletin board.

COMMUNITY ISSUES

Discuss with other students: Sometimes there are limits on rights guaranteed by the First Amendment. For example, a person can't shout "Fire!" in a movie theater, and in some cities young people can't be in large groups in public places. What are some limits on First Amendment rights? What's your opinion about these limits?

UNIT SUMMARY

KEY VOCABULARY

READING	WRITING	PEOPLE	FOUNDING FATHERS	THE CONSTITUTION & BILL OF RIGHTS	ACTIONS
capital	capital	ambassador	Alexander Hamilton		advise
city	Delaware	chief executive	Benjamin Franklin	addition	appoint
dollar bill	dollar bill	citizen	Father of Our	amendment	approve
Father of Our	Father of Our	Commander-in-Chief	Country	change	declare war
Country	Country	diplomat	George Washington	Constitution	define
first	first	inventor	James Madison	Constitutional	elect
George	is	justice	John Jay	Convention	establish
Washington	New York City	lawyer	Publius	Federalist Papers	go to court
in	of	leader		First Amendment	guarantee
is	on	member	**GOVERNMENT**	freedom	inaugurate
of	President	natural-born citizen	Cabinet	freedom of	invent
on	state	non-citizen	Congress	assembly	meet
state	the	person	enforce the laws	freedom of	protect
the	United States	police	executive branch	religion	publish
United States	was	Postmaster General	explain the laws	freedom of speech	represent
was	Washington	President	federal courts	freedom of the	respect
what		representative	House of	press	serve
who		senator	Representatives	right	set up
why		Speaker of the	judicial branch	right to petition	sign
		House of	legislative branch	the government	support
		Representatives	make the laws	supreme law of	veto
		Vice President	Senate	the land	vote
		voter	Supreme Court		win
		voting member			write
		writer			

GRAMMAR

PAST TENSE: IRREGULAR VERBS

become – became	meet – met
give – gave	set up – set up
have – had	win – won
is/are – was/were	write – wrote

PAST TENSE: WAS/WERE

Washington **was** the first President.
There **were** thirteen original states.

FUNCTIONAL EXPRESSIONS

HESITATING

Let me see.
Let me think.
Let me think for a moment.

I know the answer.
I studied this.

144

THE WAR OF 1812
THE NATIONAL ANTHEM
EXPANSION
WARS IN THE 1800s
THE CIVIL WAR
ABRAHAM LINCOLN
AMENDMENTS

- **Past Tense**
- **Ordinal Numbers**

9

VOCABULARY PREVIEW

CD 2: Track 64

1. national anthem
2. the Civil War

3. Abraham Lincoln
4. Lincoln's Gettysburg Address

CD 2: Track 65

The United States and Great Britain fought against each other in the War of 1812.

During the war, the British burned the White House and the Capitol Building.

Then at night they attacked an American fort in Baltimore Harbor.

Francis Scott Key watched the battle.

He watched the American flag at the fort.

The next morning the flag was still there.

The Americans won the battle.

Francis Scott Key wrote about this in the *Star-Spangled Banner*.

The *Star-Spangled Banner* is the national anthem of the United States.

The attack on Fort McHenry

After the attack, the flag was still there.

The *Star-Spangled Banner* is the national anthem.
Francis Scott Key wrote this song about the flag of the United States.

CD 2: Tracks 66-67

Oh, say, can you see,
by the dawn's early light,
What so proudly we hailed
at the twilight's last gleaming?
Whose broad stripes and bright stars,
through the perilous fight,
O'er the ramparts we watched,
were so gallantly streaming?
And the rockets' red glare,
the bombs bursting in air,
Gave proof through the night
that our flag was still there.
Oh, say, does that star-spangled
banner yet wave
O'er the land of the free
and the home of the brave?

Firefighters display the American flag on the Pentagon in Arlington, Virginia, after the terrorist attack on September 11, 2001.

Practice reading and singing the Star-Spangled Banner with other students.

Your Native Country's National Anthem

Does your native country have a national anthem?
What's the name of the national anthem?
Who wrote it?
When do people sing it?
Sing your native country's national anthem in class.

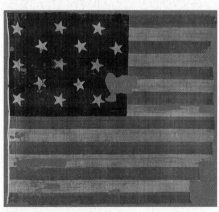
The original Star-Spangled Banner flag, National Museum of American History, Washington, D.C.

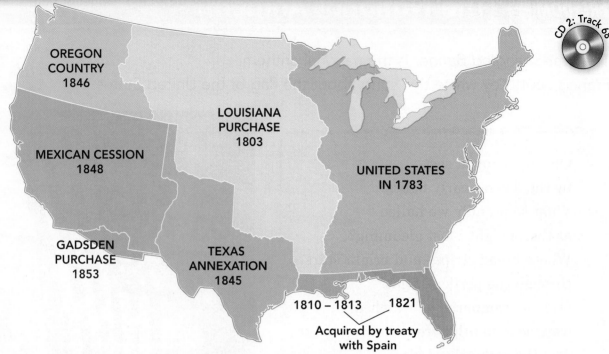

CD 2: Track 68

In the 1800s the United States expanded to the Pacific Ocean.

Americans wanted more land for homes and farms.

They wanted to use the Mississippi River to transport their farm products.

After the Revolutionary War, the western border of the United States was the Mississippi River.

The United States bought the Louisiana Territory from France in 1803.

It bought Florida from Spain in 1821.

It annexed Texas in 1845.

This led to the Mexican-American War in 1846.

The United States received the Oregon country after it signed a treaty with Great Britain in 1846.

California, Nevada, Utah, and parts of Arizona, Colorado, New Mexico, and Wyoming became part of the United States after the Mexican-American War ended in 1848.

Russia sold Alaska to the United States in 1867.

Hawaii became a territory of the United States in 1898.

(Alaska and Hawaii are the 49th and 50th states of the Union.)

The United States and Spain fought the Spanish-American War in 1898.

After that war, the United States controlled Cuba, Guam, Puerto Rico, and the Philippines.

Fact Check

| Alaska | California | Florida | Hawaii | Louisiana | Oregon |

1. The United States bought the _____ Territory from France.

2. Spain sold _____ to the United States.

3. _____ became part of the United States after the Mexican-American War.

4. Russia sold _____ to the United States.

5. Great Britain agreed to give the _____ country to the United States after the two countries signed a treaty.

6. _____ became a U.S. territory in 1898.

Civics Check

*Practice the questions and answers.**

1.	What is the name of the national anthem?	The *Star-Spangled Banner*
2.	What territory did the United States buy from France in 1803?	The Louisiana Territory Louisiana
3.	Name one war fought by the United States in the 1800s.	The War of 1812 The Mexican-American War The Civil War The Spanish-American War

* Some questions have more than one possible answer. Only one answer is required unless the question asks for more.

Your State

1. What's the name of your state? _____

2. Was your state one of the original thirteen colonies? _____

3. When did your state become a state? _____

4. Name the capital of your state. _____

5. Name a famous person in the history of your state. _____
   Why was this person famous?

The Civil War was a war between the states in the North and the states in the South.

It is also called the *War between the States*.

The North and the South fought the Civil War from 1861 to 1865.

The Northern states were also called the Union.

The Southern states were also called the Confederacy.

One main problem that led to the Civil War was slavery.

People from Africa were taken to America and sold as slaves.

They didn't have any rights or freedoms.

Their owners bought and sold them like property.

The Southern states said they needed slaves to work on the farms.

The Northern states wanted to end the system of slavery.

There were also economic reasons for the Civil War.

The North had many new factories.

The South had many big farms called plantations.

The North and the South disagreed about taxes.

These taxes helped Northern factories grow, but they made Southern farm products
more expensive overseas.

Another problem that led to the Civil War was states' rights.

The Southern states believed that state laws were more powerful than federal laws.

The Northern states believed that federal laws were more powerful than state laws.

In 1860 and 1861 eleven Southern states seceded.

They left the Union and became the Confederate states—the Confederacy.

The Civil War began in 1861.

In 1865 the North won the war.

Abraham Lincoln was the sixteenth President of the
    United States.
He led the United States during the Civil War.
He was the leader of the Northern states during the war.
Lincoln wanted to save the Union.
He wanted the Northern and Southern states to stay
    together.

Lincoln was against slavery.
In 1863 he signed the Emancipation Proclamation.
This document freed the slaves.

In 1865 the North won the Civil War.
Five days after the war ended, President Lincoln was assassinated.

Abraham Lincoln was a great President.
He preserved the Union.
Americans celebrate Presidents' Day in February each year.
On this national holiday, Americans honor George Washington and Abraham Lincoln.

Lincoln at Antietam, Maryland, 1862

The Lincoln Memorial, Washington, D.C.

Vocabulary Check

| Confederacy | plantations | rights | slavery | Union |

1. The Northern states wanted to end the system of _____.

2. The Southern states were also called the _____.

3. There were many _____ in the South.

4. Slaves didn't have any _____.

5. The _____ won the Civil War.

Fact Check

Circle the correct answer.

1. In the Northern states many people worked   in factories   on plantations   .

2. Eleven   Northern   Southern   states seceded from the Union in 1860 and 1861.

3. The   Declaration of Independence   Emancipation Proclamation   freed the slaves.

4. The Northern states believed that   federal   state   laws were more powerful than

    federal   state   laws.

5. The Civil War ended in   1861   1865   .

The Answer Is "Abraham Lincoln!"

Practice these questions and write the answers.

1. Who was the President during the Civil War?   _____

2. Who was the 16th President of the United States?   _____

3. Who led the United States during the Civil War?   _____

4. Who freed the slaves?   _____

5. Who saved the Union?   _____

Matching: *Expressions*

_____ 1. the Northern states   a. the Confederacy

_____ 2. the Southern states   b. the Civil War

_____ 3. the War between the States   c. the Union

Matching: *Reasons for the Civil War*

_____ 1. The North and the South disagreed about taxes.   a. slavery

_____ 2. The North and the South disagreed about the power of federal and state laws.   b. economic reasons

_____ 3. People from Africa who worked on Southern plantations didn't have rights or freedoms.   c. states' rights

Civics Check

Practice the questions and answers.*

CD 3: Track 1

1.	Name the U.S. war between the North and the South.	The Civil War The War between the States
2.	Name one problem that led to the Civil War.	Slavery Economic reasons States' rights
3.	What group of people was taken to America and sold as slaves?	Africans People from Africa
4.	What was one important thing that Abraham Lincoln did?	He freed the slaves. He signed the Emancipation Proclamation. He saved the Union. He preserved the Union. He led the United States during the Civil War.
5.	What did the Emancipation Proclamation do?	It freed the slaves. It freed slaves in the Confederacy. It freed slaves in the Confederate states. It freed slaves in most Southern states.
6.	Name one war fought by the United States in the 1800s.	The War of 1812 The Civil War The Mexican-American War The Spanish-American War

* Some questions have more than one possible answer. Only one answer is required unless the question asks for more.

CD 3: Track 2

Abraham Lincoln was an excellent speaker.
He gave his most famous speech in Gettysburg, Pennsylvania, in 1863.
He spoke at the dedication of the Gettysburg National Cemetery.
Four months before this speech, 51,000 Union and Confederate soldiers
  died there, or were wounded or missing, in the Battle of Gettysburg.

Lincoln's speech is called the Gettysburg Address.
It is one of the most important voices of freedom in the history of the nation.
These are the two most famous parts of Lincoln's address.

"Four score and seven years ago
our fathers brought forth on this continent,
a new nation, conceived in liberty,
and dedicated to the proposition
that all men are created equal."

" . . . (W)e here highly resolve
that these dead shall not have died in vain—
that this nation, under God,
shall have a new birth of freedom—
and that government
of the people,
by the people,
for the people,
shall not perish from the earth."

* For enrichment and speaking practice. Not required for the citizenship test.

Amendments to the Constitution

An amendment is a change to the Constitution.
It is an addition to the Constitution.
The Constitution has 27 amendments.

The first ten amendments are the Bill of Rights.
The Bill of Rights gives rights and freedoms to all people in the United States.

The First Amendment gives Americans many important rights and freedoms.
It guarantees freedom of speech.
(Americans can say what they want to.)
It guarantees freedom of the press.
(Americans can write what they want to.)
It guarantees freedom of religion.
(Americans can worship as they want to.
    They can practice any religion, or not practice a religion.)
It guarantees freedom of assembly.
(Americans can meet together as they want to.)
It guarantees the right to petition the government.
(Americans can ask the government to do something, or not do something,
    by giving the government a signed document called a petition.)

Other amendments to the Constitution are very important.
Soon after the Civil War, there were three amendments.
The 13th Amendment ended slavery.
The 14th Amendment made all Blacks citizens of the United States.
The 15th Amendment gave Blacks the right to vote.

In 1913 the 16th Amendment established income taxes.
In 1920 the 19th Amendment gave women the right to vote.
In 1964 the 24th Amendment ended the poll tax that citizens in some states
    had to pay to vote in a national election.
In 1971 the 26th Amendment gave citizens eighteen years old and older
    the right to vote.
Citizens have to be eighteen and older to vote for the President.

*Susan B. Anthony was a civil rights leader. She fought
for women's rights. In 1869 Susan B. Anthony and
Elizabeth Cady Stanton began an organization that
fought for women's suffrage—the right to vote.*

Ordinal Numbers

1st first	**11th** eleventh	**21st** twenty-first
2nd second	**12th** twelfth	**22nd** twenty-second
3rd third	**13th** thirteenth	**30th** thirtieth
4th fourth	**14th** fourteenth	**40th** fortieth
5th fifth	**15th** fifteenth	**50th** fiftieth
6th sixth	**16th** sixteenth	**60th** sixtieth
7th seventh	**17th** seventeenth	**70th** seventieth
8th eighth	**18th** eighteenth	**80th** eightieth
9th ninth	**19th** nineteenth	**90th** ninetieth
10th tenth	**20th** twentieth	**100th** one hundredth

Write the correct ordinal number. Then practice saying the sentences.

1. Abraham Lincoln was the _____ U.S. President.

2. George Washington was the _____ U.S. President.

3. Alaska was the _____ state to become part of the United States.

4. Hawaii was the _____ state to become part of the United States.

5. U.S. citizens can vote after their _____ birthday.

6. The _____ Amendment gave women the right to vote.

Matching

Match the numbers of the amendments and what they say about who can vote.

_____ 1. 26th   **a.** A male citizen of any race can vote.

_____ 2. 15th   **b.** Any citizen (women and men) can vote.

_____ 3. 24th   **c.** Citizens 18 and older can vote.

_____ 4. 19th   **d.** You don't have to pay a poll tax to vote.

Vocabulary Check

| age | income | poll | right | slavery | women |

1. The 13th Amendment ended _____.

2. The 19th Amendment gave _____ the right to vote.

3. The 16th Amendment established _____ taxes.

4. The minimum voting _____ in the U.S. is eighteen.

5. The 15th Amendment gave Blacks the _____ to vote.

6. The 24th Amendment ended the _____ tax.

Civics Check

CD 3: Track 4

*Practice the questions and answers.**

1.	What is an amendment?	A change to the Constitution An addition to the Constitution
2.	What do we call the first ten amendments to the Constitution?	The Bill of Rights
3.	What is one right or freedom from the First Amendment?	Freedom of speech Freedom of religion Freedom of assembly Freedom of the press The right to petition the government
4.	How many amendments does the Constitution have?	Twenty-seven (27)
5.	How old do citizens have to be to vote for President?	Eighteen (18) and older
6.	There are four amendments to the Constitution about who can vote. Describe one of them.	Citizens eighteen (18) and older can vote. You don't have to pay a poll tax to vote. Any citizen can vote. (Women and men can vote.) A male citizen of any race can vote.
7.	What did Susan B. Anthony do?	She fought for women's rights. She fought for civil rights.

* Some questions have more than one possible answer. Only one answer is required unless the question asks for more.

Talking Time Line: Important Dates in U.S. History

Write these events on the correct lines in the time line below.

The Bill of Rights was added to the Constitution.

The Civil War ended.

Representatives wrote the Constitution.

Women got the right to vote.

The Civil War began.

President Lincoln signed the Emancipation Proclamation.

The United States bought the Louisiana Territory.

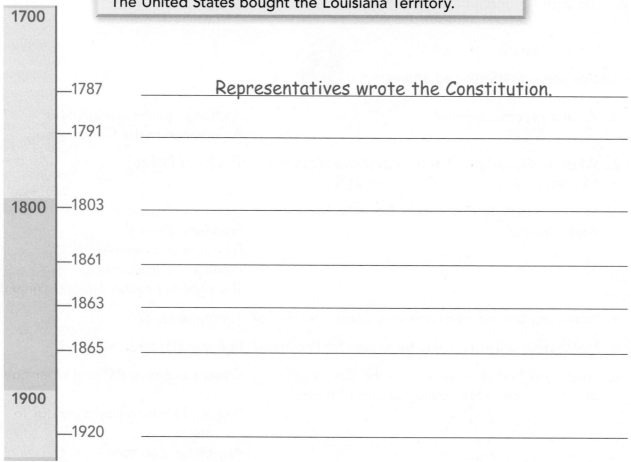

1700

—1787   Representatives wrote the Constitution.

—1791   _____

1800 —1803   _____

—1861   _____

—1863   _____

—1865   _____

1900

—1920   _____

Now practice with another student. Ask and answer questions based on the time line.

When did _____?

What happened in _____?

What should you say when you want to hear part of a question again?
You can ask about that part of the question.
You can ask the person to repeat the question.
When you ask, you can also say:
    I'm not sure I heard the question correctly.
    I'm not sure I heard that correctly.

Practice with other students. Take turns asking and answering the questions. Practice what to say when you want to hear part of a question again.

CD 3: Track 5

A. What did Susan B. Anthony do?

B. I'm sorry. What was the person's name?

A. Susan B. Anthony.

B. _____*

A. Name one war fought by the United States in the 1800s.

B. Did you say the 1800s?

A. Yes.

B. _____*

A. What is one right or freedom from the First Amendment?

B. I'm sorry. I'm not sure I heard the question correctly. Did you say the Declaration of Independence?

A. No. That's a different question.

B. Could you repeat the question, please?

A. Certainly. What is one right or freedom from the First Amendment?

B. I understand. _____*

> She fought for women's rights.
> She fought for civil rights.

> The War of 1812.
> The Mexican-American War.
> The Civil War.
> The Spanish-American War.

> Freedom of speech.
> Freedom of religion.
> Freedom of assembly.
> Freedom of the press.
> The right to petition the government.

* Some questions have more than one possible answer. Only one answer is required unless the question asks for more.

A. CIVICS

Practice the questions and answers.*

1.	What is the name of the national anthem?	The *Star-Spangled Banner*
2.	What territory did the United States buy from France in 1803?	The Louisiana Territory Louisiana
3.	Name one war fought by the United States in the 1800s.	The War of 1812 The Mexican-American War The Civil War The Spanish-American War
4.	Name the U.S. war between the North and the South.	The Civil War The War between the States
5.	Name one problem that led to the Civil War.	Slavery States' rights Economic reasons
6.	What group of people was taken to America and sold as slaves?	Africans People from Africa
7.	What was one important thing that Abraham Lincoln did?	He freed the slaves. He signed the Emancipation Proclamation. He saved the Union. He preserved the Union. He led the United States during the Civil War.
8.	What did the Emancipation Proclamation do?	It freed the slaves. It freed slaves in the Confederacy. It freed slaves in the Confederate states. It freed slaves in most Southern states.
9.	What is an amendment?	A change to the Constitution An addition to the Constitution
10.	What do we call the first ten amendments to the Constitution?	The Bill of Rights
11.	What is one right or freedom from the First Amendment?	Freedom of speech Freedom of the press Freedom of religion The right to petition Freedom of assembly the government
12.	How many amendments does the Constitution have?	Twenty-seven (27)
13.	How old do citizens have to be to vote for President?	Eighteen (18) and older

* Some questions have more than one possible answer. Only one answer is required unless the question asks for more.

14.	There are four amendments to the Constitution about who can vote. Describe one of them.	Citizens eighteen (18) and older can vote. You don't have to pay a poll tax to vote. Any citizen can vote. (Women and men can vote.) A male citizen of any race can vote.
15.	What did Susan B. Anthony do?	She fought for women's rights. She fought for civil rights.

B. KEY VOCABULARY

Write the correct word to complete the civics fact.

Alaska	flag	North	South

1. The *Star-Spangled Banner* is about the _____ of the United States.

2. Russia sold _____ to the United States in 1867.

3. During the Civil War, the states in the _____ were called the Union.

4. During the Civil War, the states in the _____ were called the Confederacy.

C. READING AND WRITING

CD 3: Tracks 6-10

Say the question. Then listen and write the sentence you hear.

1. When is Presidents' Day?

   _____

   CD 3: Track 6

2. When was Abraham Lincoln the President?

   _____

   CD 3: Track 7

3. What is one right in the Bill of Rights?

   _____

   CD 3: Track 8

4. Who can vote for the President?

   _____

   CD 3: Track 9

5. What is the largest state in the United States?

   _____

   CD 3: Track 10

Civics Enrichment

CIVIC PARTICIPATION

Work with a small group of students. Look at a copy of the U.S. Constitution. Find the amendments that you studied in this unit. Then discuss ideas for a new amendment to the Constitution. As a group, propose one new amendment to the class. Give reasons why you think this new amendment is important.

DEBATE ACTIVITY

Have a classroom debate about the voting age in the United States. Divide into two teams. Each team should take one of these positions:
  a) The minimum voting age in the United States should be 18, as it is now.
  b) The minimum voting age should be 21.

INTERNET ACTIVITY

Visit some historic places online! Go to these National Park Service websites:
www.nps.gov/fomc/—Fort McHenry National Monument, Maryland
www.nps.gov/gett/—Gettysburg National Military Park, Pennsylvania
www.nps.gov/linc/—Lincoln Memorial, Washington, D.C.

UNIT SUMMARY

KEY VOCABULARY

READING
Abraham
  Lincoln
Bill of Rights
can
for
in
is
largest
one
President
Presidents'
  Day
right
state
the
United States
vote
was
what
when
who

WRITING
Abraham Lincoln
Alaska
can
citizens
Civil War
during
February
for
freedom of
  speech
have
in
is
largest
of
one
people
President
Presidents' Day
right
state
the
United States
vote
was

PEOPLE
Abraham Lincoln
Blacks
(the) British
citizens
firefighter
Francis Scott Key
George Washington
leader
slave
soldier
Susan B. Anthony
women

EVENTS
Battle of Gettysburg
Civil War
Emancipation Proclamation
Gettysburg Address
Mexican-American War
Presidents' Day
Revolutionary War
September 11, 2001
Spanish-American War
terrorist attack
War Between the States
War of 1812

PLACES/GEOGRAPHY
Africa
Alaska
Arlington, Virginia
Baltimore Harbor
border
California
Florida
France
Gettysburg National
  Cemetery
Great Britain
Hawaii
Lincoln Memorial
Louisiana Territory
Mexico
Mississippi River
(the) North
Oregon
Pacific Ocean
Pentagon
Russia
(the) South
Spain
Texas
United States
western border

OTHER WORDS
civil rights
Confederacy
Confederate states
economic reasons
factory
farm products
federal laws
freedoms
land
national anthem
national election
native country
plantation
property
rights
slavery
Star-Spangled Banner
state laws
states' rights
taxes
territory
treaty
Union
women's rights
women's suffrage

GRAMMAR

PAST TENSE: IRREGULAR VERBS

become – became	have – had	sell – sold
begin – began	lead – led	speak – spoke
buy – bought	leave – left	win – won
fight – fought	make – made	write – wrote
give – gave	say – said	

FUNCTIONAL EXPRESSIONS

ASKING FOR REPETITION
I'm not sure I heard the question correctly.
I'm not sure I heard that correctly.
Could you repeat the question, please?

CLARIFYING
Did you say . . . ?

INDICATING UNDERSTANDING
I understand.

INDUSTRIAL REVOLUTION
LABOR MOVEMENT
IMMIGRATION
20th-CENTURY HISTORY
CIVIL RIGHTS MOVEMENT
SEPTEMBER 11, 2001

- **Past Tense**

VOCABULARY PREVIEW

CD 3: Track 17

1. invention
2. labor movement
3. immigration
4. the Great Depression
5. the United Nations
6. civil rights movement

This unit describes some of the most important events and people in modern U.S. history. Some of the information is required for the citizenship test, and some is not. Use the Civics Check activities in the unit to practice the specific information you need for the test.

The first Americans were farmers.

In the 1790s the first factories opened in the United States.

The cotton gin and the sewing machine were very important inventions.

With these machines, the United States produced clothing much faster than before.

Americans also invented the telephone, the typewriter, the phonograph, and the light bulb.

The railroads went across the country from the East Coast to the West Coast.

The factories were usually in cities, and the cities grew larger.

People came from the farms and immigrants came from other countries to work in the factories.

CD 3: Track 12

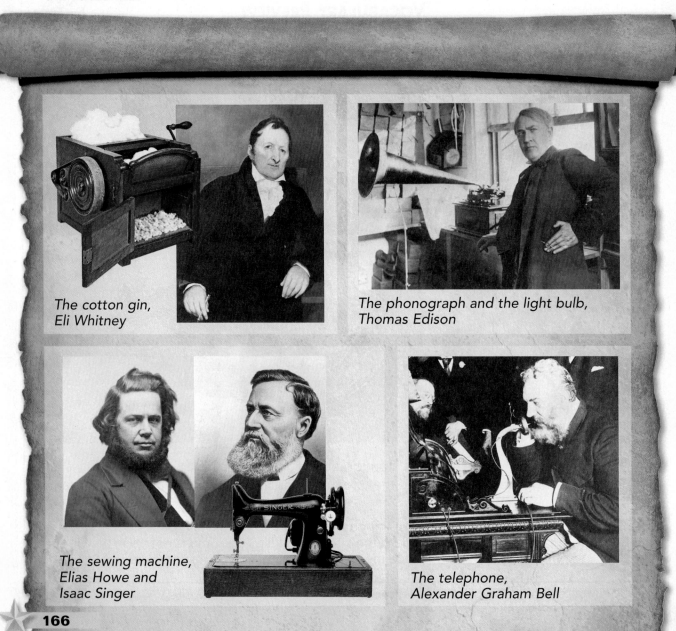

The cotton gin,
Eli Whitney

The phonograph and the light bulb,
Thomas Edison

The sewing machine,
Elias Howe and
Isaac Singer

The telephone,
Alexander Graham Bell

The Labor Movement

CD 3: Track 13

Factory workers had a difficult life.

They usually worked twelve hours a day.

Their pay was low.

Many workers got hurt because the factories weren't safe.

Workers began to come together in groups.

They formed labor unions.

These unions fought for better hours, better pay, and safer workplaces.

Many workers belong to unions today.

Americans celebrate Labor Day every year on the first Monday in September.

This national holiday celebrates the workers of the United States.

Clothing workers demonstrating for better labor conditions

Labor Day parade, New York City, 1909

167

In the 1800s America grew very quickly.

Expansion added new farmland, and the Industrial Revolution built new factories and cities.

America needed farmers and workers.

Immigrants came from many countries.

They worked on farms and in factories.

They helped build the cities of the United States.

In the 1900s the United States began to limit immigration.

The government made many laws to stop immigration from many countries.

In 1965 a new immigration law changed this.

The law allowed immigrants to apply from any country.

Immigrants continue to come to the United States every day.

Some come here because life was difficult or dangerous in their native country.

Others come here because they want a better life for themselves and their families here in the United States.

Except for Native Americans, *all* Americans come from families of immigrants.

The United States is "a nation of immigrants."

Vocabulary Check

| clothing | holiday | immigrants | labor unions | laws | sewing machine |

1. The _____ was a very important invention.

2. Workers formed _____ to fight for better hours and better pay.

3. America's farms and factories needed _____ from other countries in the 1800s.

4. In the 1900s the country made _____ to limit immigration.

5. With new machines, American factories produced _____ much faster than before.

6. Labor Day is a national _____ in September.

Did You Understand?

1. Name one important invention during the Industrial Revolution.

2. Why did workers form labor unions?

3. Why did the United States need immigrants in the 1800s?

Discussion

1. Where did people work in your native country in the place where you lived?
   On farms? In factories? In offices?
   What did you do in your native country before you came to the United States?

2. If you are working now, tell about your job. What are your hours?
   Is your pay good? Is your workplace safe? Is there a union?
   What can you do to make your workplace safer or better?

3. Why did you come to the United States? How did you get here? Did you come alone or with your family? What did you do when you first came here?

World War I

CD 3: Track 15

World War I began in 1914.

The United Kingdom,* France, and Russia
fought Germany and Austria-Hungary.

The United States entered World War I in 1917
and helped the United Kingdom, France, and
Russia win the war.

Woodrow Wilson was the President during
World War I.

The war ended in 1918.

The United States became a great world power.

The Depression

From 1929 to 1939 there was a Great
Depression.

The American economy collapsed.

The Depression had many causes.

Factories and farms produced too much.

After World War I, countries in Europe didn't
have money to buy American goods.

Many people borrowed too much money.

It was a very difficult time in the United States.

Factories closed, workers lost their jobs or
their salaries were cut, many banks closed,
and many people lost all their money in the
stock market.

* The United Kingdom = The United Kingdom of
Great Britain and Ireland (during World War I)

Franklin Delano Roosevelt

CD 3: Track 16

Franklin D. Roosevelt was the President
of the United States from 1933 to 1945.
He became the President during the Great
Depression.
His plan to help the country was called the
New Deal.
The government made jobs for people who had
no work.
They built roads, parks, bridges, and buildings.
The government gave people loans to help them
keep their farms or homes.
The Social Security system began.

Roosevelt was the President during World War II.
He served longer than any other President.
He died during his fourth term in office in 1945.

World War II

World War II began in 1939.
The United States, the United Kingdom,* Russia,
and other countries were called the Allied
nations.
They fought Japan, Germany, and Italy.
The United States entered World War II in 1941
when the Japanese bombed Pearl Harbor in
Hawaii.
In 1945 the United States dropped two atomic
bombs on Hiroshima and Nagasaki in Japan.
The United States and the Allied nations won the
war in 1945.

General Dwight D. Eisenhower was the leader of
the Allied forces in Europe during World War II.
Later he became the President of the United States.

* The United Kingdom = The United Kingdom of
Great Britain and Northern Ireland (since 1927)

The United Nations (The UN)

After World War II, many countries
formed a new international
organization called the United Nations.
It is also called the UN.*
At the United Nations, countries discuss world
problems and try to keep peace.
The UN also helps many countries.
It gives them economic aid and provides
education programs, health programs, and
other assistance.

The Cold War, the Korean War, and the Vietnam War

After World War II, the United States and the
Soviet Union became major world powers.
The two countries had very different political
systems.
The American system is democratic, and the
Soviet system was communist.
The United States and the Soviet Union did not
fight each other directly in a war, but they
competed with each other politically and
economically.
This was called the Cold War.
During the Cold War, the main concern of the
United States was Communism.

The United States fought Communist forces in
two wars.
From 1950 to 1953, the United States fought in
the Korean War.
From 1964 to 1973, the United States fought in
the Vietnam War.
The Cold War ended during the years 1990 and
1991 when the Soviet Union broke up into
independent states.

* UN is pronounced "U-N."

The Persian Gulf War

CD 3: Track 18

The Persian Gulf War began in 1990 when Iraq invaded Kuwait.

The United States entered the war in 1991.

The military forces of the United States, the United Kingdom, and 32 other nations were called the coalition forces.

The war ended quickly in 1991 when the Iraqi forces left Kuwait.

George H.W. Bush was the President during the Persian Gulf War.

In the United States, the Persian Gulf War was also called Operation Desert Storm.

Wars Fought by the United States in the 1900s

World War I

World War II

The Korean War

The Vietnam War

The Persian Gulf War

J Check-Up

Vocabulary Check

Depression	United Nations	Cold War	World War I	New Deal

1. The _____ is the international organization formed after World War II.

2. Woodrow Wilson was the President during _____.

3. The _____ was Franklin D. Roosevelt's plan to help the country.

4. From 1929 to 1939 there was a Great _____.

5. The United States and the Soviet Union competed during the _____.

Did You Understand?

1. What happened during the Great Depression? Why?
2. What was the New Deal?
3. When did the United States enter World War II? (After what event?)
4. What was the major difference between the American and Soviet political systems?
5. What is the UN?
6. When did the Persian Gulf War begin? (After what event?)

Fact Check

Circle the correct answer.

1. The United States fought in the   Korean   Vietnam   War from 1964 to 1973.

2.   Social Security   The Vietnam War   began when Franklin D. Roosevelt was the President.

3. The U.S. economy collapsed during the   Depression   Cold War .

4. The United States fought Germany, Italy, and   Russia   Japan   during World War II.

5. The Soviet Union had a   democratic   communist   political system.

Matching: *Presidents and Events*

____ **1.** Franklin D. Roosevelt   **a.** was the President during World War I.

____ **2.** George H.W. Bush   **b.** led the Allied forces in Europe during World War II.

____ **3.** Woodrow Wilson   **c.** was the President during World War II.

____ **4.** Dwight D. Eisenhower   **d.** was the President during the Persian Gulf War.

Listening

Listen and circle the correct answer.

1.
   a. Woodrow Wilson
   b. Franklin D. Roosevelt

2.
   a. Woodrow Wilson
   b. Franklin D. Roosevelt

3.
   a. Japan
   b. The United Kingdom

4.
   a. The New Deal
   b. The United Nations

5.
   a. The Great Depression
   b. Communism

6.
   a. Dwight D. Eisenhower
   b. George H.W. Bush

Civics Check

Practice the questions and answers.*

1. Name one war fought by the United States in the 1900s.	World War I World War II The Korean War The Vietnam War The (Persian) Gulf War
2. Who was President during World War I?	(Woodrow) Wilson
3. Who was President during the Great Depression and World War II?	(Franklin) Roosevelt
4. Who did the United States fight in World War II?	Japan, Germany, and Italy
5. Before he was President, Eisenhower was a general. What war was he in?	World War II
6. During the Cold War, what was the main concern of the United States?	Communism

* Some questions have more than one possible answer. Only one answer is required unless the question asks for more.

The Civil Rights Movement

During the 1950s and 1960s, the civil rights movement worked to end racial discrimination against Blacks in the United States.
It worked for equal rights for all Americans.

The Reverend Martin Luther King, Jr., was the most famous leader of the civil rights movement.
He fought for civil rights.
He worked for equality for all Americans.
He led protests against discrimination in many states.
In 1963 he led hundreds of thousands of people in a demonstration to support new civil rights laws.
It was called the March on Washington.

In 1968 Martin Luther King, Jr., was shot and killed.
The civil rights movement and the nation lost a great leader.
The United States remembers Martin Luther King, Jr., in a national holiday on the third Monday in January every year.

During the March on Washington in 1963, Martin Luther King, Jr., gave a very powerful and beautiful speech at the Lincoln Memorial.

It is called his "I Have a Dream" speech.

These are the most famous parts of what he said that day.

> I . . . have a dream. It is a dream deeply rooted in the American dream. I have a dream that one day this nation will rise up and live out the true meaning of its creed: "We hold these truths to be self-evident—that all men are created equal."
>
> This will be the day when all of God's children will be able to sing with new meaning "My Country 'tis of thee, sweet land of liberty, of thee I sing. Land where my fathers died, land of the pilgrim's pride, from every mountainside let freedom ring." And if America is to be a great nation this must become true.
>
> When we let freedom ring, when we let it ring from every village and every hamlet, from every state and every city, we will be able to speed up that day when all of God's children, black men and white men, Jews and Gentiles, Protestants and Catholics, will be able to join hands and sing in the words of the Old Negro spiritual, "Free at last! Free at last! Thank God almighty, we are free at last!"

* For enrichment and speaking practice. Not required for the citizenship test.

September 11, 2001

On the morning of September 11, 2001, terrorists attacked the United States.
They hijacked four airplanes from Boston, New Jersey, and the Washington, D.C. area.
They crashed two planes into the twin towers of the World Trade Center in New York City.
Both towers of the World Trade Center collapsed.
One plane crashed into the Pentagon—the headquarters of the United States military, in Arlington, Virginia.
One plane crashed in a field in Pennsylvania.
Thousands of people died in the buildings and on the airplanes.
People from more than eighty different countries died in the attacks.
Most of the victims were Americans.

The U.S. government asked other nations to join in a fight against terrorism around the world.
President George W. Bush ordered air attacks against Afghanistan.
Then he sent American troops there to fight against the terrorist organization responsible for the attacks on the United States.

Vocabulary Check

| demonstration | discrimination | equality | holiday | speech |

1. The civil rights movement tried to end racial _____.

2. Martin Luther King, Jr., worked for _____ for all Americans.

3. The United States remembers Martin Luther King, Jr., in a national

   _____ in January.

4. Martin Luther King, Jr., led a _____ called the March on Washington in 1963.

5. He gave his famous "I Have a Dream" _____ at the Lincoln Memorial.

Civics Check

Practice the questions and answers. *

CD 3: Track 24

1. What movement tried to end racial discrimination?	The civil rights movement
2. What did Martin Luther King, Jr., do?	He fought for civil rights. He worked for equality for all Americans.
3. What major event happened on September 11, 2001, in the United States?	Terrorists attacked the United States.

* Some questions have more than one possible answer. Only one answer is required unless the question asks for more.

Discussion

1. How do you think the civil rights movement of the 1950s and 1960s helps immigrants in the United States today?

2. In your opinion, is there still discrimination in the United States? Give reasons for your answer.

Talking Time Line: Important Dates in U.S. History

Write these events on the correct lines in the time line below.

Martin Luther King, Jr., led a civil rights march in Washington.
The Great Depression began in the United States.
The Korean War ended.
The United States entered World War I.
World War II ended.
Japan bombed Pearl Harbor.
Terrorists attacked the United States.
Martin Luther King, Jr., was killed.

1900	
—1917	<u>The United States entered World War I.</u>
—1929	_____
—1941	_____
—1945	_____
1950 —1953	_____
—1963	_____
—1968	_____
2000 —2001	_____

Now practice with another student. Ask and answer questions based on the time line.

When did _____?

What happened in _____?

CD 3: Track 25

Practice with other students. Take turns asking and answering the questions. Practice what to say when you want to hear part of a question again.

A. Who was President during World War I?

B. Excuse me. Did you say World War II?

A. No. World War I. The First World War.

B. _____

> (Woodrow) Wilson.

A. Name one war fought by the United States in the 1900s.

B. I'm not sure I heard correctly. Did you say the 1800s or the 1900s?

A. The 1900s.

B. I understand. _____ *

> World War I.
> World War II.
> The Korean War.
> The Vietnam War.
> The (Persian) Gulf War.

A. Who did the United States fight in World War II?

B. World War II?

A. Yes.

B. _____, _____, and . . . hmm . . .

I know there's one more country. Oh yes. _____.

A. That's correct.

> Japan
> Germany
> Italy

* Some questions have more than one possible answer. Only one answer is required unless the question asks for more.

A. CIVICS

Practice the questions and answers.*

1.	Name one war fought by the United States in the 1900s.	World War I World War II The Korean War The Vietnam War The (Persian) Gulf War
2.	Who was President during World War I?	(Woodrow) Wilson
3.	Who was President during the Great Depression and World War II?	(Franklin) Roosevelt
4.	Who did the United States fight in World War II?	Japan, Germany, and Italy
5.	Before he was President, Eisenhower was a general. What war was he in?	World War II
6.	During the Cold War, what was the main concern of the United States?	Communism
7.	What movement tried to end racial discrimination?	The civil rights movement
8.	What did Martin Luther King, Jr., do?	He fought for civil rights. He worked for equality for all Americans.
9.	What major event happened on September 11, 2001, in the United States?	Terrorists attacked the United States.

* Some questions have more than one possible answer. Only one answer is required unless the question asks for more.

B. CIVICS MATCHING

Match the sentence parts.

_____ 1. Martin Luther King, Jr.   a. was President during World War II.

_____ 2. George H.W. Bush   b. was President during the Persian Gulf War.

_____ 3. Dwight D. Eisenhower   c. led the civil rights movement.

_____ 4. Franklin D. Roosevelt   d. was President during World War I.

_____ 5. Woodrow Wilson   e. led the Allied forces in Europe during World War II.

C. KEY VOCABULARY

Write the correct word to complete the civics fact.

come	Labor Day	people	rights
September	United States	Washington	

1. During the Great Depression many _____ lost their jobs.

2. _____ is a holiday that celebrates the workers of the United States.

3. Many immigrants _____ to the United States for a better life.

4. Martin Luther King, Jr., worked for civil _____.

5. The March on _____ was in 1963.

6. Labor Day is in _____.

7. The Soviet Union and the _____ competed during the Cold War.

D. READING AND WRITING

Say the question. Then listen and write the sentence you hear.

1. When is Labor Day?

_____

CD 3: Track 26

2. Why do people come to the United States?

_____

CD 3: Track 27

3. Name one right people in the United States have.

_____

CD 3: Track 28

4. What can citizens of the United States do?

_____

CD 3: Track 29

5. Who can citizens of the United States vote for?

_____

CD 3: Track 30

Civics Enrichment

Visit the Franklin Institute online to learn about these famous inventors!
http://sln.fi.edu/franklin/inventor/bell.html—Alexander Graham Bell
http://sln.fi.edu/franklin/inventor/edison.html—Thomas Edison
http://sln.fi.edu/franklin/inventor/inventor.html—Benjamin Franklin

Visit Ellis Island online! More than 12 million immigrants entered the U.S. through this immigration station between 1892 and 1954. Go to www.nps.gov/elis/ and click on "Photos & Multimedia" to see a slideshow and photos of this historic site.

Have a classroom debate about civil rights in the United States today. Divide into two teams. Each team should take one of these positions:
   a) The election of President Obama shows that discrimination in the U.S. has ended.
   b) Despite the election of President Obama, discrimination in the U.S. continues today.

UNIT SUMMARY

KEY VOCABULARY

READING	WRITING	PEOPLE	EVENTS/HISTORICAL PERIODS	PLACES/GEOGRAPHY	OTHER WORDS
can	and	American	civil rights movement	Afghanistan	Allied Nations
citizens	be	Blacks	Cold War	Arlington, Virginia	atomic bomb
come	can	Dwight D.	Great Depression	Austria-Hungary	civil rights
do	citizens	Eisenhower	Industrial Revolution	Europe	coalition forces
for	come	factory worker	Korean War	France	communist
have	for	farmer	Labor Day	Germany	democratic
in	free	Franklin D.	March on Washington	Hawaii	discrimination
is	freedom of	Roosevelt	national holiday	Hiroshima	equal rights
Labor Day	speech	general	New Deal	Iraq	equality
name	have	George H.W.	Operation Desert	Italy	factory
of	in	Bush	Storm	Kuwait	farmland
one	is	immigrant	Persian Gulf War	Japan	immigration
people	Labor Day	(the) Japanese	September 11, 2001	Lincoln Memorial	invention
right	of	leader	Vietnam War	Nagasaki	labor movement
the	people	Native	war	New Jersey	labor union
to	President	American	World War I	New York City	military forces
United States	Senators	President	World War II	Pearl Harbor	native country
vote	September	Martin Luther		Pennsylvania	political system
what	the	King, Jr.	**INVENTIONS**	Pentagon	racial discrimination
when	to	terrorist	cotton gin	Russia	railroad
who	United States	troops	light bulb	Soviet Union	Social Security system
why	vote	worker	phonograph	United Kingdom	stock market
			sewing machine	United Nations	terrorism
			telephone	United States	terrorist organization
			typewriter	Washington, D.C.	union
				World Trade Center	United Nations (UN)

GRAMMAR

PAST TENSE: IRREGULAR VERBS

become – became	get hurt – got hurt	lead – led
begin – began	give – gave	lose – lost
break up – broke up	go – went	make – made
build – built	grow – grew	send – sent
come – came	have – had	shoot – shot
fight – fought		

FUNCTIONAL EXPRESSIONS

CLARIFYING
Excuse me. Did you say ___?
I'm not sure I heard correctly.
   Did you say ___ or ___?

INDICATING UNDERSTANDING
I understand.

HESITATING
. . . hmm . . .
I know *there's one
more country.*
Oh yes.

NATIONAL HOLIDAYS
U.S. PRESIDENTS

- ## Present Tense: Review
- ## Past Tense

11

VOCABULARY PREVIEW

CD 3: Track 31

1. Martin Luther King, Jr. Day
2. Memorial Day
3. Independence Day
4. Labor Day
5. Veterans Day
6. Thanksgiving Day

This unit offers information about some of our most important U.S. Presidents. Some of the information is required for the citizenship test, and some is not. Use the Civics Check activities in the unit to practice the specific information you need for the test.

CD 3: Track 32

New Year's Day is on January 1st.

Martin Luther King, Jr. Day is in January. On this holiday we remember the important civil rights leader.

Presidents' Day is in February. This holiday celebrates the birthdays of George Washington and Abraham Lincoln.

Memorial Day is in May. On this day we honor the men and women who gave their lives during service in the U.S. military.

Independence Day is also called the Fourth of July. It celebrates the day that the American colonies declared their independence.

Labor Day is in September. This holiday celebrates the workers of the United States.

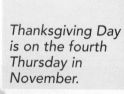

Columbus Day is in October.

Veterans Day is in November. It honors all men and women who served in the U.S. military.

Thanksgiving Day is on the fourth Thursday in November.

Christmas is on December 25th.

Writing Check I

Write the correct month to complete each sentence.

1. Labor Day is in _____.

2. Columbus Day is in _____.

3. Presidents' Day is in _____.

4. Thanksgiving is in _____.

5. Memorial Day is in _____.

6. Independence Day is in _____.

7. Flag Day is in _____.

> We celebrate Flag Day on June 14th. On that day in 1777, the colonies passed the Flag Resolution. This established the flag's stars-and-stripes design. Flag Day isn't an official national holiday. People go to work on that day.

Writing Check II

Write the correct U.S. holiday next to each month.

1. February   _____

2. May   _____

3. June   _____

4. July   _____

5. September   _____

6. October   _____

7. November   _____

Columbus Day

Flag Day

Independence Day

Labor Day

Memorial Day

Presidents' Day

Thanksgiving

Civics Check

CD 3: Track 33

Practice the questions and answers.

1. When do we celebrate Independence Day?	July 4 (fourth)	
2. Name two national U.S. holidays.*	New Year's Day	Labor Day
	Martin Luther King, Jr. Day	Columbus Day
	Presidents' Day	Veterans Day
	Memorial Day	Thanksgiving
	Independence Day	Christmas

* Important: You must name *two* holidays when you answer this question.

CD 3: Track 34

George Washington

George Washington became the first President
   of the United States in 1789.
He was the leader of the Colonial Army during the
   Revolutionary War.
He was the leader of the Constitutional Convention in 1787.
He served two terms as President.
We call him the *Father of Our Country*.

John Adams

John Adams was the second President.
He served as President from 1797 to 1801.
Before that, he was George Washington's Vice President.
Adams was an important Founding Father.
Before the Revolutionary War, he wrote articles to protest
   British taxes and laws.
He helped the colonies write their constitutions and set up
   their governments.
He organized support for the Declaration of Independence
   in the colonies.

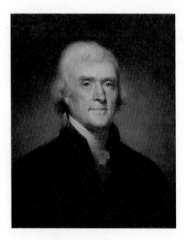

Thomas Jefferson

Thomas Jefferson was the third President.
He served as President from 1801 to 1809.
He was one of the most important Founding Fathers.
He wrote the Declaration of Independence.
He was the first Secretary of State.
During his presidency, the United States bought the
   Louisiana Territory from France.

Thomas Jefferson died on the Fourth of July in 1826—
   exactly 50 years after the adoption of the Declaration of
   Independence.
John Adams died on the same day just a few hours later.

James Madison

CD 3: Track 35
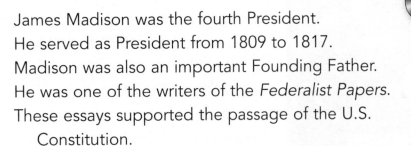

James Madison was the fourth President.
He served as President from 1809 to 1817.
Madison was also an important Founding Father.
He was one of the writers of the *Federalist Papers*.
These essays supported the passage of the U.S. Constitution.
He also wrote the amendments that became the Bill of Rights—the first ten amendments to the Constitution.

Abraham Lincoln

Abraham Lincoln was the sixteenth President.
He served as President from 1861 to 1865.
He led the United States during the Civil War.
He saved the Union.
He signed the Emancipation Proclamation.
This document freed the slaves.
Five days after the Civil War ended, Lincoln was assassinated.

Woodrow Wilson

Woodrow Wilson was the 28th President.
He served as President from 1913 to 1921.
He was the President during World War I.
He worked to create the League of Nations, an international organization.
Women got the right to vote during his time in office.

Franklin D. Roosevelt

Franklin D. Roosevelt was the 32nd President.

He served from 1933 to 1945—longer than any other President.

He was the President during the Great Depression.

His plan to help the country was called the *New Deal*.

He was the President during World War II.

He died during his fourth term in office in 1945.

Dwight D. Eisenhower

Dwight D. Eisenhower was the 34th President.

He served as President from 1953 to 1961.

Before he was President, he was a general.

He was the leader of the Allied forces in Europe during World War II.

He began the interstate highway system.

During his time in office, the Soviet Union launched the first *Sputnik* satellite into space.

The "space race" began between the United States and the Soviet Union.

John F. Kennedy

John F. Kennedy was the 35th President.

He served as President from 1961 to 1963.

He worked for civil rights.

He wanted to begin many programs to help poor people.

He began the Peace Corps—a program that sends American volunteers to help in developing countries around the world.

He sent soldiers to Vietnam.

He expanded the U.S. space program.

President Kennedy was assassinated in 1963.

Lyndon B. Johnson

Lyndon B. Johnson was the 36th President.

He became President in 1963 after Kennedy's assassination.

He served as President until 1969.

His *Great Society* programs helped poor people.

These programs included Medicaid (a health-care program for the poor) and Medicare (a health-care program for senior citizens).

Important civil rights laws were passed during his administration.

The Vietnam War expanded during his time in office.

Richard Nixon

Richard Nixon was the 37th President.

He served as President from 1969 to 1974.

He began relations with China, and he improved relations with the Soviet Union.

He ended the United States' role in Vietnam.

He resigned because of a political scandal called Watergate.

Gerald Ford

Gerald Ford was the 38th President.

He was the first President not elected as President or Vice President by the people.

He became President in 1974 when Nixon resigned.

He served as President until 1977.

The nation's economy was bad during his time in office.

James Earl (Jimmy) Carter

Jimmy Carter was the 39th President.
He served as President from 1977 to 1981.
He worked for human rights for people in foreign
   countries.
He worked for peace in the Middle East.
He didn't have experience in national politics.
The nation's economy didn't get better during his time in
   office.

Ronald Reagan

Ronald Reagan was the 40th President.
He served as President from 1981 to 1989.
He lowered taxes and spent more money on the military.
He worked to reduce the role of the federal government
   in regulating business, providing social services, and
   other aspects of U.S. life.
The nation's economy improved during his two terms.
Before he entered politics, Ronald Reagan was an actor.
As President, he was called "the great communicator."

George H.W. Bush

George H.W. Bush was the 41st President.
He served as President from 1989 to 1993.
Before that, he was Ronald Reagan's Vice President.
He continued many of the Reagan policies.
In 1991 he sent troops to the Persian Gulf War, also called
   Operation Desert Storm.
There was a recession during his time in office.
The economy was very bad.

William J. (Bill) Clinton

Bill Clinton was the 42nd President.

He served as President from 1993 to 2001.

He raised taxes, reformed the welfare system, and eliminated the national debt.

He increased federal money for schools and local police departments.

He sent troops to Somalia, Bosnia, and Kosovo to support international peace-keeping missions.

He was involved in political and personal scandals.

In 1998 he was impeached by the House of Representatives.

In 1999 the Senate had an impeachment trial.

President Clinton was acquitted and stayed in office.

George W. Bush

George W. Bush was the 43rd President.

He is the son of former President George H.W. Bush.

He served as President from 2001 to 2009.

On September 11, 2001, eight months after he took office, international terrorists attacked the United States.

President Bush declared a "War on Terrorism."

In 2001 he sent U.S. troops to Afghanistan to fight the terrorist organization responsible for the attacks on the United States.

In 2003 he sent U.S. troops to Iraq to remove the country's weapons of mass destruction and to remove Iraq's leader Saddam Hussein.

The weapons weren't found, and the decision to invade Iraq was controversial.

During his time in office, income taxes were cut and schools were required to test students more often to improve the education system.

The U.S. economy entered a long recession in the last year of the Bush presidency.

CD 3: Track 39

Barack H. Obama

Barack Obama was the 44th President.
He served as President from 2009 to 2017.
He was the first African-American President.
Before he became President, he was a U.S. senator from Illinois.
As President Obama took office, the U.S. economy was in a long recession and the country was at war in Iraq and Afghanistan.
During his time in office, the recession ended and the economy improved.
The government raised taxes on wealthy Americans and lowered taxes for people with low incomes.
The wars in Iraq and Afghanistan continued, but most U.S. troops returned home.
The nation's health care system was reformed during his presidency and the number of Americans with health insurance increased.
President Obama is a member of the Democratic Party.
(The two major political parties in the United States are the Democratic and Republican parties.)

Donald J. Trump

Donald J. Trump is the 45th President.
He became President in January 2017.
He is a businessman and TV personality from New York.
He ran for office with a campaign to *Make America great again.*
He plans to improve the economy, reform the health care system, create new jobs, spend more money on the military, and lower taxes.
He wants to change immigration laws and reduce the role of the federal government in regulating business.
President Trump is a member of the Republican Party.

Civics Check

CD 3: Track 41

*Practice the questions and answers.**

1.	Who was the first President?	(George) Washington
2.	Who is the "Father of Our Country"?	(George) Washington
3.	Who wrote the Declaration of Independence?	(Thomas) Jefferson
4.	What territory did the United States buy from France in 1803?	The Louisiana Territory Louisiana
5.	The Federalist Papers supported the passage of the U.S. Constitution. Name one of the writers.	(James) Madison (John) Jay (Alexander) Hamilton Publius
6.	What was one important thing that Abraham Lincoln did?	He freed the slaves. He signed the Emancipation Proclamation. He saved the Union. He preserved the Union. He led the United States during the Civil War.
7.	What did the Emancipation Proclamation do?	It freed the slaves. It freed slaves in the Confederacy. It freed slaves in the Confederate states. It freed slaves in most Southern states.
8.	Who was President during World War I?	(Woodrow) Wilson
9.	Who was President during the Great Depression and World War II?	(Franklin) Roosevelt
10.	Before he was President, Eisenhower was a general. What war was he in?	World War II
11.	What major event happened on September 11, 2001, in the United States?	Terrorists attacked the United States.
12.	What is the name of the President of the United States now?	(Donald) Trump Donald J. Trump
13.	What is the name of the Vice President of the United States now?	(Mike) Pence Michael R. Pence
14.	What is the political party of the President now?	The Republican Party Republican
15.	What are the two major political parties in the United States?	Democratic and Republican

* Some questions have more than one possible answer. Only one answer is required unless the question asks for more.

UNIT TEST

A. CIVICS

Practice the questions and answers.*

1.	When do we celebrate Independence Day?	July 4 (fourth)
2.	Name two national U.S. holidays.** ** Important: You must name *two* holidays when you answer this question.	New Year's Day Labor Day Martin Luther King, Jr. Day Columbus Day Presidents' Day Veterans Day Memorial Day Thanksgiving Independence Day Christmas
3.	Who was the first President?	(George) Washington
4.	Who is the "Father of Our Country"?	(George) Washington
5.	Who wrote the Declaration of Independence?	(Thomas) Jefferson
6.	What territory did the United States buy from France in 1803?	The Louisiana Territory Louisiana
7.	The Federalist Papers supported the passage of the U.S. Constitution. Name one of the writers.	(James) Madison (John) Jay (Alexander) Hamilton Publius
8.	What was one important thing that Abraham Lincoln did?	He freed the slaves. He signed the Emancipation Proclamation. He saved the Union. He preserved the Union. He led the United States during the Civil War.
9.	What did the Emancipation Proclamation do?	It freed the slaves. It freed slaves in the Confederacy. It freed slaves in the Confederate states. It freed slaves in most Southern states.
10.	Who was President during World War I?	(Woodrow) Wilson
11.	Who was President during the Great Depression and World War II?	(Franklin) Roosevelt
12.	Before he was President, Eisenhower was a general. What war was he in?	World War II
13.	What major event happened on September 11, 2001, in the United States?	Terrorists attacked the United States.
14.	What is the name of the President of the United States now?	(Donald) Trump Donald J. Trump

* Some questions have more than one possible answer. Only one answer is required unless the question asks for more.

196

15.	What is the name of the Vice President of the United States now?	(Mike) Pence Michael R. Pence
16.	What is the political party of the President now?	The Republican Party Republican
17.	What are the two major political parties in the United States?	Democratic and Republican

B. KEY VOCABULARY

Write the correct month to complete the civics fact.

1. Americans celebrate Presidents Lincoln and Washington in _____.

2. A holiday in _____ celebrates workers.

3. Families come together and celebrate Thanksgiving in _____.

4. The American colonies declared their independence in _____.

5. We celebrate the flag on a holiday in _____.

C. READING AND WRITING

Say the question. Then listen and write the sentence you hear.

1. When is Memorial Day?

_____

CD 3: Track 42

2. When is Independence Day?

_____

CD 3: Track 43

3. When is Thanksgiving?

_____

CD 3: Track 44

4. When is Columbus Day?

_____

CD 3: Track 45

5. When is Flag Day?

_____

CD 3: Track 46

CIVIC PARTICIPATION

What is your favorite national holiday in the United States? Why? How do you celebrate it? Share with the class.

INTERNET ACTIVITY

Learn about U.S. Presidents online. Go to www.whitehouse.gov and click on "About the White House." Select "Presidents" and then click on a President's name to get information. You can also see a slideshow about the Presidents. Click on "About the White House," select "White House 101," and click on "Our Presidents" to begin the slideshow.

PROJECT

Biography Project: Write a short biography about a President of the United States. Use your school library or local library to find information, or use the White House website. Give a short presentation to the class.

UNIT SUMMARY

KEY VOCABULARY

READING/WRITING: HOLIDAYS

Presidents' Day
Memorial Day
Flag Day
Independence
  Day
Labor Day
Columbus Day
Thanksgiving

MONTHS

February
May
June
July
September
October
November

OTHER

in
is
when

PRESIDENTS

John Adams
George H.W. Bush
George W. Bush
Jimmy Carter
Bill Clinton
Dwight D.
  Eisenhower
Gerald Ford
Thomas Jefferson
Lyndon B. Johnson
John F. Kennedy
Abraham Lincoln
James Madison
Richard Nixon
Barack Obama
Ronald Reagan
Franklin D.
  Roosevelt
Donald Trump
George Washington
Woodrow Wilson

PEOPLE

actor
businessman
civil rights leader
Founding Father
general
leader
member
men
poor people
President
Secretary of State
senior citizens
slave
soldier
terrorist
troops
TV personality
U.S. senator
Vice President
volunteer (n.)
women
worker
writer

NATIONAL HOLIDAYS

Christmas
Columbus Day
Flag Day
Independence Day
Labor Day
Martin Luther King, Jr.
  Day
Memorial Day
New Year's Day
Presidents' Day
Thanksgiving Day
Veterans Day

PLACES/GEOGRAPHY

Afghanistan
Bosnia
China
Europe
France
Illinois
Iraq
Kosovo
Louisiana Territory
Middle East
Somalia
Soviet Union
Vietnam

EVENTS/HISTORICAL PERIODS

Civil War
Great Depression
Great Society
  programs
impeachment trial
New Deal
Operation Desert
  Storm
Persian Gulf War
recession
Revolutionary War
September 11, 2001
Vietnam War
War on Terrorism
Watergate
World War I
World War II

DOCUMENTS

Bill of Rights
Constitution
Declaration of
  Independence
Emancipation
  Proclamation
Federalist Papers

GRAMMAR

PAST TENSE: IRREGULAR VERBS

become – became	do – did	is/are – was/were	spend – spent
begin – began	get – got	lead – led	take – took
buy – bought	give – gave	send – sent	write – wrote

CITIZENS' RIGHTS
CITIZENS' RESPONSIBILITIES
PARTICIPATING IN OUR
DEMOCRACY
THE OATH OF ALLEGIANCE

- **Can**
- **Should**
- **Must**
- **Will**

12

VOCABULARY PREVIEW

CD 3: Track 47

1. obey the law
2. pay taxes

3. serve on a jury
4. register for the Selective Service

5. vote
6. the oath of allegiance

Citizens' Rights

Everyone living in the United States has many rights.

Freedom of expression
(Freedom of speech)   *Freedom of assembly*   *Freedom of religion*

Freedom to petition the government   *The right to bear arms*

Some rights are only for United States citizens.

The right to vote in a federal election   *The right to run for federal office*

Every four years in November, citizens can vote for President of the United States.

Citizens have to be 18 and older to vote for President.

They usually choose between a Democratic and a Republican candidate for
President.

The Democratic and Republican parties are the two major political parties in the
United States.

Whose Rights?

Circle the correct answer.

1. Freedom of expression — everyone   citizens

2. Freedom of religion — everyone   citizens

3. The right to vote in a federal election — everyone   citizens

4. The right to bear arms — everyone   citizens

5. Freedom of assembly — everyone   citizens

6. The right to run for federal office — everyone   citizens

Matching

_____ 1. freedom of assembly 　　 a. Citizens can be candidates in a federal election.

_____ 2. freedom of religion 　　 b. Americans can own firearms.

_____ 3. the right to run for office 　　 c. Americans can say what they want to.

_____ 4. freedom of expression 　　 d. Americans can worship as they want to.

_____ 5. the right to bear arms 　　 e. Americans can meet together as they want to.

Civics Check

Practice the questions and answers.

CD 3: Track 49

1.	What are two rights of everyone living in the United States?* * Important: You must give *two rights* when you answer this question.	Freedom of expression (Freedom of speech) Freedom to petition the government Freedom of assembly Freedom of religion The right to bear arms
2.	Name one right only for United States citizens.	(The right to) vote in a federal election (The right to) run for federal office
3.	How old do citizens have to be to vote for President?	Eighteen (18) and older
4.	What are the two major political parties in the United States?	Democratic and Republican

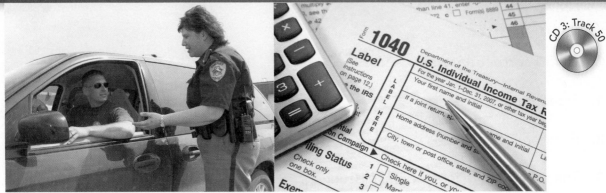

People in the United States have rights, and they also have responsibilities.

People should obey the law.

The "rule of law" is a basic principle of American democracy.

Everyone must follow the law.

No one is above the law.

People in the United States should pay taxes.

They should send in federal income tax forms and pay income taxes.

April 15 is usually the last day you can send in federal income tax forms.

In many states, people also pay state income taxes.

In some cities and counties, people also pay local income taxes.

Men in the United States must serve in the military if they are needed.

All men must register for the Selective Service at age eighteen—citizens and non-citizens.

Men who are older than age eighteen when they enter the United States must register before their 26th birthday.

Some responsibilities are only for United States citizens.

Citizens should serve on a jury.

Citizens should vote in a federal election.

Check-Up

Vocabulary Check

| jury | law | register | taxes | vote |

1. Everyone should obey the _____.

2. Citizens should serve on a _____.

3. April 15 is the last day you can pay federal _____.

4. At age 18 men must _____ for the Selective Service.

5. Citizens should _____ in elections.

Civics Check

CD 3: Track 51

*Practice the questions and answers.**

1. What is the "rule of law"?	Everyone must follow the law. Leaders must obey the law. Government must obey the law. No one is above the law.
2. When is the last day you can send in federal income tax forms?	April fifteen (15)
3. What is one responsibility that is only for United States citizens?	Serve on a jury Vote in a federal election
4. When must all men register for the Selective Service?	At age eighteen (18) Between eighteen (18) and twenty-six (26) ** ** This is the official civics test answer. However, men must actually register before their 26th birthday.

* Some questions have more than one possible answer. Only one answer is required unless the question asks for more.

Discussion

1. What taxes do you pay? How does the government use the money?
2. Why is the "rule of law" important?
3. Why should people vote in elections?
4. In your opinion, what is the most important *right* that Americans have? Why?
5. In your opinion, what is the most important *responsibility* that Americans have? Why?

203

You can participate in our democracy in many ways.

CD 3: Track 52

You can vote.

You can join a political party.

You can help with a campaign.

You can join a civic group.

You can call your senators and representatives.

You can give an elected official your opinion on an issue.

You can run for office.

You can write to a newspaper.

You can publicly support or oppose an issue or policy.

Check-Up

Vocabulary Check

campaign	opinion	oppose	run	write

1. You can give an elected official your _____.

2. You can publicly support or _____ a policy.

3. You can _____ to a newspaper.

4. You can help with a _____.

5. You can _____ for office.

Civics Check

CD 3: Track 53

*Practice the question and answers.**

What are two ways that Americans can participate in their democracy?	Vote. Join a political party. Help with a campaign. Join a civic group. Join a community group. Give an elected official your opinion on an issue. Call senators and representatives. Publicly support or oppose an issue or policy. Run for office. Write to a newspaper.

* Important: When you answer this question, you must give *two* answers.

Discussion

1. What civic groups are there in your community?
   Which civic group do you want to join? Why?

2. What issue or policy do you support?
   What issue or policy do you oppose?
   How can you express your opinions?

3. What are other ways that you can participate in our democracy?

The Oath of Allegiance

CD 3: Track 54

You will become a citizen of the United States at a naturalization ceremony. During the ceremony, you will recite an oath of allegiance to the United States. When you recite the oath, you will make these promises.

I promise to give up loyalty to other countries.

I promise to defend the Constitution and laws of the United States.

I promise to obey the laws of the United States.

I promise to serve in the U.S. military if needed.

I promise to serve the nation if needed.

I promise to do important work for the nation if needed.

I promise to be loyal to the United States.

A naturalization ceremony at Monticello, the home of Thomas Jefferson in Virginia

Members of the U.S. military at their naturalization ceremony while serving in Iraq

The Oath of Allegiance

I hereby declare, on oath,

that I absolutely and entirely renounce and abjure all allegiance and fidelity to any foreign prince, potentate, state, or sovereignty, of whom or which I have heretofore been a subject or citizen;

that I will support and defend the Constitution and laws of the United States of America against all enemies, foreign and domestic;

that I will bear true faith and allegiance to the same;

that I will bear arms on behalf of the United States when required by the law;

that I will perform noncombatant service in the Armed Forces of the United States when required by the law;

that I will perform work of national importance under civilian direction when required by the law;

and that I take this obligation freely without any mental reservation or purpose of evasion; so help me God.

Civics Check

CD 3: Track 56

Practice the question and answers.*

What is one promise you make when you become a United States citizen?	Give up loyalty to other countries. Defend the Constitution and laws of the United States. Obey the laws of the United States. Serve in the U.S. military (if needed). Serve the nation (if needed). Do important work for the nation (if needed). Be loyal to the United States.

* Some questions have more than one possible answer. Only one answer is required unless the question asks for more.

Practice with other students. Take turns asking and answering the questions.

CD 3: Track 57

A. What are two rights of everyone living in the United States?

B. Did you say *everyone*?

A. Yes, everyone—citizens and non-citizens.

B. _____* and . . . let me see . . .

_____.

Freedom of expression (Freedom of speech)	Freedom to petition the government
	Freedom of religion
Freedom of assembly	The right to bear arms

A. What is one responsibility that is only for United States citizens?

B. I'm sorry. Did you say one *right* or one *responsibility*?

A. One responsibility.

B. _____

Serve on a jury.	Vote in a federal election.

A. What are two ways that Americans can participate in their democracy?

B. Could you please repeat the question?

A. Sure. Americans can participate in their democracy in many ways. Tell me two ways.

B. I see. _____ and . . . let me think for

a moment . . . _____.

Vote	Give an elected official your opinion on an issue
Join a political party	Call senators and representatives
Help with a campaign	Publicly support or oppose an issue or policy
Join a civic group	Run for office
Join a community group	Write to a newspaper

* Some questions have more than one possible answer. Only one answer is required unless the question asks for more.

A. CIVICS: Rights and Responsibilities

Practice the questions and answers.*

1.	What are two rights of everyone living in the United States?** ** Important: You must give *two* answers.	Freedom of expression Freedom of speech Freedom of assembly Freedom to petition the government Freedom of religion The right to bear arms
2.	Name one right only for United States citizens.	(The right to) vote in a federal election (The right to) run for federal office
3.	How old do citizens have to be to vote for President?	Eighteen (18) and older
4.	What are the two major political parties in the United States?	Democratic and Republican
5.	When is the last day you can send in federal income tax forms?	April fifteen (15)
6.	What is one responsibility that is only for United States citizens?	Serve on a jury Vote in a federal election
7.	When must all men register for the Selective Service?	At age eighteen (18) Between eighteen (18) and twenty-six (26)
8.	What are two ways that Americans can participate in their democracy?** ** Important: You must give *two* answers.	Vote. Join a political party. Help with a campaign. Join a civic group. Join a community group. Give an elected official your opinion on an issue. Call senators and representatives. Publicly support or oppose an issue or policy. Run for office. Write to a newspaper.
9.	What is one promise you make when you become a United States citizen?	Give up loyalty to other countries. Defend the Constitution and laws of the United States. Obey the laws of the United States. Serve in the U.S. military (if needed). Serve the nation (if needed). Do important work for the nation (if needed). Be loyal to the United States.

* Some questions have more than one possible answer. Only one answer is required unless the question asks for more.

B. CIVICS: Principles of American Democracy Review

Practice the questions and answers.*

1.	What is the supreme law of the land?	The Constitution
2.	What does the Constitution do?	It sets up the government. It defines the government. It protects basic rights of Americans.
3.	The idea of self-government is in the first three words of the Constitution. What are these words?	We the People
4.	What is an amendment?	A change to the Constitution An addition to the Constitution
5.	What do we call the first ten amendments to the Constitution?	The Bill of Rights
6.	What is one right or freedom from the First Amendment?	Freedom of speech Freedom of religion Freedom of assembly Freedom of the press The right to petition the government
7.	How many amendments does the Constitution have?	Twenty-seven (27)
8.	What did the Declaration of Independence do?	It announced our independence from Great Britain. It declared our independence from Great Britain. It said that the United States is free from Great Britain.
9.	What are two rights in the Declaration of Independence?** ** Important: You must give *two* answers.	Life Liberty The pursuit of happiness
10.	What is freedom of religion?	You can practice any religion, or not practice a religion.
11.	What is the economic system in the United States?	A capitalist economy A market economy
12.	What is the "rule of law"?	Everyone must follow the law. Leaders must obey the law. Government must obey the law. No one is above the law.

* Some questions have more than one possible answer. Only one answer is required unless the question asks for more.

C. KEY VOCABULARY

Write the correct word to complete the civics fact.

| flag | free | pay | right | Senator | taxes | United States |

1. April 15 is the last day to _____ federal taxes.

2. Citizens have the _____ to vote in a federal election.

3. When you become a citizen, you promise to be loyal to the _____.

4. People in the United States have to pay _____.

5. After the Revolutionary War, the American colonies were _____ from Great Britain.

6. When we say the Pledge of Allegiance, we show loyalty to the _____ of the United States.

7. To participate in our democracy, you can call your _____ and give your opinion.

D. READING AND WRITING

Say the question. Then listen and write the sentence you hear.

1. What do people in the United States pay to the government?

   _____

   CD 3: Track 58

2. What is one right citizens of the United States have?

   _____

   CD 3: Track 59

3. Who can citizens vote for?

   _____

   CD 3: Track 60

4. Who elects the President?

   _____

   CD 3: Track 61

5. What do people in the United States have to pay?

   _____

   CD 3: Track 62

Civics Enrichment

CIVIC PARTICIPATION

Where do people in your community vote on Election Day? What local officials do people vote for? What happens at the polling places? What do the voting machines look like? How do people register to vote? Get information from your local Board of Elections. As a class, visit a polling place on Election Day.

COMMUNITY ISSUES

Discuss: What are the rights and responsibilities of all people in their communities and in the nation? How are these rights and responsibilities different for citizens and non-citizens?

DEBATE ACTIVITY

Have a classroom debate about the right to vote. Only *citizens* have the right to vote for the President, senators, and representatives in *federal* elections. Should *non-citizens* have the right to vote in *local* elections in their cities and towns? Divide into two teams. Each team should take one of these positions:
  a) Non-citizens should have the right to vote in local elections.
  b) Non-citizens shouldn't have the right to vote in local elections.

UNIT SUMMARY

KEY VOCABULARY

READING	WRITING	RIGHTS
can	and	freedom of assembly
citizens	can	freedom of expression
do	citizens	freedom of speech
elects	Congress	freedom of religion
for	elect	freedom to petition the
government	for	government
have	have	right to bear arms
in	in	right to run for federal
is	of	office
of	pay	right to vote
one	people	
pay	President	**RESPONSIBILITIES**
people	right	obey the law
President	taxes	pay taxes
right	the	register for the Selective
the	to	Service
to	United States	rule of law
United States	vote	serve on a jury
vote		vote
what		
who		

PARTICIPATING IN OUR DEMOCRACY

call your senators and representatives
give an elected official your opinion on an
   issue
help with a campaign
join a civic group
join a political party
publicly support or oppose an issue or policy
run for office
vote
write to a newspaper

OATH OF ALLEGIANCE

be loyal to the United States
defend the Constitution and laws of the
   United States
do important work for the nation if needed
give up loyalty to other countries
obey the laws of the United States
recite an oath of allegiance
serve in the U.S. military if needed
serve the nation if needed

GRAMMAR

CAN

Citizens **can** vote for
   President.

SHOULD

People **should** obey
   the law.

MUST

All men **must** register for
   the Selective Service.

WILL

I **will** support and defend
   the Constitution.

FUNCTIONAL EXPRESSIONS

CLARIFYING

Did you say ___?
I'm sorry. Did you say ___ or ___?

ASKING FOR REPETITION

Could you please repeat the
   question?

HESITATING

Let me see.
Let me think for a
   moment.

What to Bring

- [ ] The appointment letter from USCIS telling you when and where to appear for your interview
- [ ] Your permanent resident card or alien registration card
- [ ] Your passport (even if it has expired)
- [ ] Your driver's license or state identification card
- [ ] Any reentry permits you have
- [ ] Any other documents listed on your appointment letter
- [ ] Two *additional* passport-size photographs

Important:
You *must* contact USCIS beforehand if you can't go to your interview.
If you reschedule your interview for a later date, you might have to wait several months for a new appointment.
If you don't go to your interview and you don't contact USCIS beforehand, USCIS will "administratively close" your case and you will have to "reopen" your case within one year.

Arriving at the USCIS Office

Go to the USCIS office at least 30 minutes before the time of your interview. You might go through a security checkpoint to enter the office.

A. Do you have an appointment?
B. Yes. I have an appointment for my interview for citizenship.
A. Please put your bag on the conveyor belt, put any metal objects in the tray, and step through the metal detector.
B. Okay.

Checking In

At some USCIS offices, you might check in at a reception counter.

A. I'm here for my citizenship interview.
B. What's your name?
A. _____
B. Okay. Please take a seat in the waiting area. Listen for your name. The officer will come out to meet you.
A. Thank you.

THE ENGLISH TEST (Speaking)

1. Greeting the USCIS Officer

Your English test might begin in the waiting area! The USCIS officer will call your name. When you hear your name, stand up and greet the officer.

A. _____(your name)_____?

B. Yes. I'm _____(your name)_____.

A. I'll be conducting your interview today.

B. Nice to meet you.

A. Nice meeting you, too. Please follow me.

B. Okay.

2. Walking to the Office

As you walk to the office, the officer might ask you some questions. Be ready to have a simple "small talk" conversation. Relax and be friendly!

A. How are you today?

B. I'm fine, thanks. How are you?

A. Fine.

A. How did you get here today?

B. { I _____. (took the bus / took the subway / drove / walked)
My ___(family member)___ brought me by car.

A. How long did it take to get here?

B. { It took about ____ minutes.
It took about an hour.

(Other possible questions: How was the traffic? Did you have trouble parking? Was the bus on time?)

A. How's the weather outside?

B. It's _____. (sunny / raining / cloudy / cold / cool / warm / hot)

A. How do you like the weather today?

B. { I like it. It's _____.
I don't like it. It's _____.

A. Is it still raining?

B. Yes, it is. / No. It stopped raining.

A. Is it still cloudy?

B. Yes, it is. / No. It's sunny now.

A. Did anyone come with you today?

B. { Yes. My _____. (husband / wife / . . . / friend)
No. I'm here by myself.

A. Are you nervous?

B. I'm a little nervous.

A. Have you been preparing for your interview?

B. Yes. I've been studying English and U.S. history and government.

A. Have you been going to a school?

B. { Yes. I go / went to ___(name of school)___.
No. I studied at home by myself.

(If you went to school, other possible questions: How many days a week did you go to school? What was your teacher's name? Did you like your class?)

3. Swearing In

The officer might ask you to sit down for a moment and then to stand up again.

A. { Please have a seat while I get your file.
{ Please sit down while I get out your information.
B. Thank you.

A. Please stand and raise your right hand.
Do you solemnly swear to tell the truth, the whole truth, and nothing but the truth?
B. I do.
A. Please be seated.
Do you understand what you just promised to do?
B. Yes. I promised that all the information I give will be true. I won't lie.

Or the officer might swear you in immediately.

A. Please remain standing. Raise your right hand.
Do you solemnly affirm that the statements you are about to make will be the truth, the whole truth, and nothing but the truth?
B. I do.
A. Do you understand what that means?
B. Yes. I promise to tell the truth. All the information I give will be true. I won't lie.
A. { Please be seated.
{ Please take a seat.
{ Please have a seat.
{ You may sit down.
B. Thank you.

4. Presenting Your Identification

The officer will ask to see your identification at the beginning of the interview. Have all your forms of identification on the desk or in your hand so they are ready to show immediately.

A. { May I see your identification?
{ Do you have your forms of identification?
B. Yes. Here's my _____ and my
_____.
(permanent resident card / alien registration card /
passport / driver's license / state identification card)
A. And did you also bring two passport-size photographs?
B. Yes. Here they are.

The officer might ask a question about your identification.

A. Is this your current driver's license / state identification card?
B. Yes, it is.

A. Is this your most recent passport? I see that it has expired.
B. Yes. It has expired now. It's my most recent passport.

About the English Speaking Test

The USCIS officer will evaluate your English speaking ability through your answers to questions about the information on your Form N-400 (Application for Naturalization). The officer will have your Form N-400 information during the interview. Prepare to answer questions about any information on the form. Especially prepare to talk about any unusual information on your form or any information that has changed since you completed the form.

Always tell the truth!

If you want the officer to repeat a question, say:

Could you please say that again?
Could you please repeat that?
Could you repeat that, please?
Could you please say that again more slowly?
Could you repeat that more slowly, please?

You can say "I'm sorry" or "Excuse me" before any of these sentences. For example:

I'm sorry. Could you please say that again?
Excuse me. Could you please repeat that?

Be confident and proud during your interview!

Sit up straight in your chair.
Make eye contact with the officer. (Don't look down too much.)
Answer all questions using words. (Don't just move your head or your shoulders
   to give an answer or to say you don't know an answer.)
Don't be too nervous.
Smile!
Be friendly!

As you study these pages, write your information on the blank lines and practice conversations with a partner.

5. Giving Your Name

The officer will probably ask about your name.

A. What's your family name/last name/surname?
B. _____

A. What's your given name/first name?
B. _____

A. And what's your full middle name?
_____

A. What's your full name?
B. _____
   (Give first, middle, and last name.)

A. Is your family name/last name/surname
   _____?

B. { Yes, it is.
    { No, it isn't. It's _____.

The officer might ask about other names you reported on the N-400 form.

A. Have you ever used other names?

B. { No.
{ Yes. I have used the name _____.

A. According to your N-400 form, you haven't ever used another name. Is that correct?

B. Yes. That's correct. I've never used another name.

A. According to your N-400 form, you have also used the name _____. Is that correct?

B. Yes. That's correct. _____ (Explain.)

The officer might ask about changing your name. (Write the new name on a piece of paper and bring it to the interview.)

A. { Do you want to legally change your name?
{ Do you wish to change your name at this time?

B. { No.
{ Yes. The new name I want to use is _____.

6. Giving Information about Your Eligibility

*This information is important for your citizenship eligibility.**

A. { How long have you been a lawful permanent resident of the United States?
{ How long have you been a permanent resident?

B. For _____ years.

A. Are you married to a U.S. citizen?

B. { No.
{ Yes. My husband/wife has been a U.S. citizen for _____ years.**

* To become a citizen, you must be at least 18 years old. You must be a permanent resident for at least five years, or you must be a permanent resident for at least three years and married to and living with the same U.S. citizen for the last three years.

** If you answer "Yes," the officer might ask: "Have you lived with your husband/wife continuously for the last three years?" If true, the correct answer is "Yes."

7. Giving Information about Yourself

The officer might ask for this information. Or the officer might say some information and ask if it is correct. If it is correct, say "Yes." If it is wrong, say "No" and give the correct information.

1.	A. What's your social security number? B. My social security number is _____.	A. Is your social security number _____? B. { Yes. { No. My social security number is _____.
2.	A. What's your date of birth? B. My date of birth is __(month/day/year)__.	A. Is your birth date _____? B. { Yes. { No. My birth date is _____.
3.	A. When were you born? B. I was born on _____.	A. Were you born on _____? B. { Yes. { No. I was born on _____.

4.	A. { When did you become a permanent
	     resident?
	   { On what date did you become a
	     permanent resident?
	B. On _____.
		A. Did you become a permanent resident on
		   _____?
		B. { Yes.
		{ No. On _____.

5.	A. { Where were you born?
	   { In what country were you born?
	   { What's your country of birth?
	B. I was born in _____.
		A. Were you born in _____?
		B. { Yes.
		{ No. I was born in _____.

6.	A. { What's your nationality?
	   { What's your country of nationality?
	B. I'm _____.
		A. { Is your nationality _____?
		   { Is your country of nationality _____?
		B. { Yes.
		{ No. It's _____.

7.	A. Are either of your parents U.S. citizens? B. { Yes. My mother/father is a citizen. { No. A. Were your parents married before your 18th birthday? B. { Yes. { No.	A. Is your mother/father a U.S. citizen? B. { Yes. { No.

8.	A. What's your marital status?
	B. I'm _____.
	   (single/married/divorced/widowed/
	   separated)
		A. Are you _____?
		   (single/married)
		B. { Yes. I'm _____.
		{ No. I'm _____.

R7

8. Giving Information about Address and Telephone Numbers

A. What's your current address?
B. Do you mean my home address?
A. Yes—where you live now.
B. It's _____.*

(*Give full address – number, street, city, state, zip code.)

A. { Is your address still _____?
     Do you still live at _____?
     Are you still living at _____?

B. { Yes.
     No. I moved. My new address is _____.

A. What were your previous addresses during the last five years?
B. Previous addresses? I'm sorry. I don't understand. Could you please say that another way?
A. Yes. Where else have you lived? What were your old addresses?
B. I lived at _____ from ___(month/day/year)___ to ___(month/day/year)___.**

(**Be prepared to give information about your addresses for the last five years, including dates.)

A. What's your daytime phone number?
B. _____.

A. Is your daytime phone number still _____?
B. { Yes.
     No. It's _____.

A. What's your evening phone number?
B. _____.

A. Do you have a mobile phone number?
B. { A cell phone number? Yes. It's _____.
     A cell phone number? No, I don't.

A. Do you have an email address?
B. { Yes. It's _____.
     No, I don't.

9. Giving Information for Criminal Records Search

A. What's your height?/How tall are you?
B. I'm ____ feet ____ inches tall.

A. What's your weight?/How much do you weigh?
B. I weigh ____ pounds.

A. Are you Hispanic or Latino?
B. Yes./No.

A. What's your race?
B. _____.

   (White/Asian/Black (African-American)/American Indian/
   Alaskan Native/Native Hawaiian/Other Pacific Islander)

A. What's your hair color?/What color is your hair?
B. _____.

A. What's your eye color?/What color are your eyes?
B. _____.

Asking the Officer to Paraphrase a Question

If you don't understand a word or a question, you can ask the officer to *paraphrase*—to say the question using different words. First, apologize and say you don't understand:

I'm sorry. I don't understand.
I'm sorry. I don't understand the question.
I'm sorry. I didn't understand what you said.
I'm sorry. I didn't understand what you asked.

Then ask the officer to say the question a different way:

Could you please explain what that means?
Could you please explain that?
Could you please say the question another way?
Could you please ask that again using different words?
Could you please give me an example of what that means?
Could you please tell me what "_____(word)_____" means?

Put these sentences together to politely ask the officer to paraphrase. For example:

I'm sorry. I don't understand. Could you please explain what that means?

Another short way to ask for the meaning of a word is to repeat just the word and make it sound like a question. For example:

"Position?"

10. Giving Information about Your Employment and Schools You Attended

The officer might ask for information about your employment and schools separately, or the officer might ask about your employment and schools together.

A. Are you employed?
B. I'm sorry. I don't understand. Could you please tell me what "employed" means?
A. Yes. It means "working." Do you work now? Do you have a job?
B. Yes. I work.
A. What's the name of your employer?
B. _____
A. And what is your employer's address?
B. _____
A. What's your position there?
B. My "position"?
A. Yes—your occupation. What's your job?
B. I'm _____.

A. { How long have you worked there?
     { How long have you been working there?
B. For _____ weeks / months / years.
A. And what was your previous job?
B. I _____.

A. Can you name the schools you attended during the last five years?
B. Yes. I attended _____
   from _____ to _____.
A. What did you study?
B. I studied _____.
   (Answer about each school you attended.)

A. Are you employed or in school now?

B. { Yes. I work at _____. I'm a _____.
{ Yes. I'm a student at _____. I'm studying _____.

A. How long have you been there?

B. For _____ weeks/months/years.

A. What did you do before that?

B. I _____.

A. And before that?

B. I _____.

Be prepared to talk about your places of work and schools during the last five years. The officer will probably ask about your most recent work or school first.

11. Talking about Time Outside the United States

Be prepared to talk about this information. It's very important during the interview, especially if you have traveled outside the United States during the past five years.

A. { Have you been absent from the United States during the past five years?
{ Have you spent time outside the United States during the past five years?

B. { Yes, I have.
{ No, I haven't.

A. How many total days (24 hours or longer) did you spend outside the United States during the last five years?

B. I've spent ____ days outside the country.

A. How many trips of 24 hours or more have you taken outside of the United States during the past five years?

B. I've taken ____ trips. (no, 1, 2, . . .)

A. { When did you last leave the United States?
{ When was the last time you left the United States?
{ When was your most recent trip outside the United States?

B. _____ (month/day/year)

A. { How long were you away?
{ How long were you absent?
{ How long were you gone?
{ How long were you out of the United States on that trip?

B. For _____ days.

A. { Where did you go?
{ Where did you travel?

B. I went to _____.

A. { What was the reason for the trip?
{ Why?

B. _____.

A. Tell me about the trip you took outside the United States before that one.

B. *(Write sentences to describe that trip and other trips you took during the past five years. Practice the sentences so you can describe these trips during your interview.)*

_____

_____

_____

_____

How the Officer Might Ask If You Understand

The officer might ask if you understand a question:

Do you understand?

Would you like me to explain that?

Do you understand what I asked?

Should I explain that for you?

Do you know what that means?

I'm not sure you understood me.

Did you understand that?

I'm not sure you understood the question.

Did you understand me?

You can answer:

Yes.

No. I don't understand.

Yes. I understand.

No. I didn't understand.

If you don't understand a question, ask the officer to say the question a different way:

Could you please explain what that means?

Could you please explain that?

Could you please say the question another way?

Could you please ask that again using different words?

Could you please explain what that means?

Could you please explain that?

Could you please give me an example of what that means?

For example:

A. What's your spouse's name?

B. Hmm. My spouse's name?

A. Do you know what that means?

B. No. I don't understand. Could you please explain that?

A. Your spouse is your husband/wife.

B. Oh. I understand. My spouse's name is _____.

12. Giving Information about Your Marital History

Be prepared to answer these questions about Part 10 of your N-400 form.

What's your current marital status?

Are you single? married? divorced? widowed?

How many times have you been married?

When were you married?/What's the date of your marriage?

What's your wife's/husband's/spouse's name?

What's her/his citizenship?

Is she/he a U.S. citizen?

When did she/he become a U.S. citizen?

Where does your spouse work?/Who is your spouse's employer?

13. Giving Information about Your Children

Be prepared to answer these questions about Part 11 of your N-400 form.

How many children do you have?/How many sons and daughters have you had?

What are their names?

What is your oldest child's name? How old is she/he? What's her/his date of birth?

Where was she/he born? What is her/his country of birth?

What is her/his relationship to you—a biological child? a stepchild? a legally adopted child?

Does she/he live with you now?/What's her/his current address?

Tell me about your other children.

Be prepared to give this information about each child.

Answering the Form N-400 "Part 12" Questions*

The most difficult questions during your interview might be from Part 12 of the N-400 form. Many of these questions begin with the words "Have you ever . . .." These questions ask if you did something at any time in your life—as a child, in your native country, and in the United States.

The answers to most Part 12 questions are simply "Yes" or "No." But if you just answer "Yes" or "No" during your interview, the officer won't know if you understand a question and might ask, "Do you know what this question means?" So try to practice more complete answers—answers that show that you understand the questions. If you don't understand a question, you can ask the officer to say the question a different way.

14. Answering Additional Questions

Here are the Part 12 questions and some possible answers. Only use an answer if it is true for you. If your answer is different, write your answer and practice it. Always tell the truth during the interview!

1. Have you ever claimed to be a U.S. citizen?	No. I've never told anyone I am a U.S. citizen.
2. Have you ever registered to vote in any federal, state, or local election in the United States?	No. I've never registered to vote in this country. I want to be a citizen so I can vote in the future.
3. Have you ever voted in any federal, state, or local election in the United States?	No. I've never voted in an election. I want to be a citizen so I can vote in the future.
4a. Do you now have, or did you ever have, a hereditary title or an order of nobility in any foreign country?	No. I was just a regular person in my country—not a prince/princess or anything like that.
4b. At your naturalization ceremony, are you willing to give up any inherited title or order of nobility that you have in a foreign country?	Yes. I will give up that title/order, and I will be loyal only to the United States.
5. Have you ever been declared legally incompetent or been confined to a mental institution?	No. I've never had mental health problems.
6. Do you owe any overdue federal, state, or local taxes?	No. I always pay my taxes on time.
7. Have you ever not filed a federal, state, or local tax return since you became a lawful permanent resident?	No. I always send in all the required tax forms.
8. Have you called yourself a "non-U.S. resident" on a federal, state, or local tax return since you became a lawful permanent resident?	No. When I file my tax returns, I file as a resident.
9. Have you ever been a member of, involved in, or in any way associated with, any organization, association, fund, foundation, party, club, society, or similar group in the United States or in any other location in the world?**	Yes. I'm a member of _____. (the parents' association in my children's school / my church / the labor union at my work / . . .) Yes. In my country I was a member of _____. No. I haven't been a member of any group like this in the United States or in another country.
What was/is the name of the group? What was/is the purpose of the group? ** Be sure to tell about any organization. A "Yes" answer can show that you are a good member of your community.	The name is _____. (the Key School PTA / Church of the Redeemer / Local 437 / . . .) The purpose is _____.

* The *Voices of Freedom* Activity & Test Prep Workbook provides additional practice with these questions.

10. Have you ever been a member of or in any way associated with . . . the Communist Party? any other totalitarian party? a terrorist organization?	No. I am not a Communist, and I never was a Communist. I don't believe in Communism. Yes. I had to join the Communist Party to work in my former country. It was compulsory. No. I believe that dictators are bad and that people in all countries should have rights and freedoms. No. I believe that terrorism is very bad.
11. Have you ever advocated the overthrow of any government by force or violence?	No. I think violence is bad. I believe that government should change peacefully through elections.
12. Have you ever persecuted any person because of race, religion, national origin, membership in a particular social group, or political opinion?	No. I've never hurt any person in this way. I believe that people of all races, religions, and groups should have the same rights.
13. Between March 23, 1933, and May 8, 1945, did you work for or associate in any way with the Nazi government of Germany?	No. I was never a Nazi. I had no connection with that government.
14. Were you ever involved in any way with . . . a. genocide? b. torture? c. killing, or trying to kill, someone? d. badly hurting, or trying to hurt, a person on purpose? e. forcing, or trying to force, someone to have any kind of sexual contact or relations? f. not letting someone practice his or her religion?	a. No. I've never been involved in killing people. b. No. I've never been involved in hurting a person. c. No. I've never been involved in the death of a person. d. No. I've never intentionally hurt or injured a person. e. No. I've never forced a person to have sex. f. No. I believe that all people should have the right to follow their religion.
15. Were you ever a member of, or did you ever serve in, help, or otherwise participate in a military unit? a paramilitary unit? a police unit? a self-defense unit? a vigilante unit? a rebel group? a guerrilla group? a militia? an insurgent organization?	No. I've never been involved in any official or unofficial military group or any group that uses weapons or fights against a government.
16. Were you ever a worker, volunteer, or soldier, or did you otherwise ever serve in a prison or jail? a prison camp? a detention facility? a labor camp? any other place where people were forced to stay?	No. I've never worked or served in a jail or any other place where people are forced to stay or to work.
17. Were you ever a part of any group, or did you ever help any group, unit, or organization that used a weapon against any person, or threatened to do so?	No. I've never been involved with any group that hurt a person, used a gun or other weapon, or threatened a person with a weapon.
18. Did you ever sell, give, or provide weapons to any person, or help another person sell, give, or provide weapons to any person?	No. I've never been involved with providing a gun or any other weapon to another person.
19. Did you ever receive any type of military, paramilitary, or weapons training?	No. I've never received training from any official or unofficial military group, and I've never received training about how to use a gun or other weapon.
20. Did you ever recruit, enlist, conscript, or use any person under 15 years of age to serve in or help an armed force or group?	No. I've never asked, signed up, or required any child to be a soldier or part of any official or unofficial military group.
21. Did you ever use any person under 15 years of age to do anything that helped or supported people in combat?	No. I've never used a child to help people involved in war, fighting, or other military action.

224

22.	Have you ever committed, assisted in committing, or attempted to commit, a crime or offense for which you were not arrested?	No. I've never done anything that is against the law.
23.	Have you ever been arrested, cited, or detained by any law enforcement officer (including any immigration official or any official of the U.S. Armed Forces) for any reason?	No. I've never had a problem with a police officer or other officer. . Yes. _____ (*Write and practice your answer. Be sure to tell the truth. Example: A police officer gave me a ticket for not wearing my seat belt while driving.*)
24.	Have you ever been charged with committing, attempting to commit, or assisting in committing a crime or offense?	No. I've never been accused of doing anything against the law.
25.	Have you ever been convicted of a crime or offense?	No. I've never been found guilty of doing anything against the law.
26.	Have you ever been placed in an alternative sentencing or a rehabilitative program?	No. I've never done anything against the law, so I've never been placed in a program like this.
27.	Have you ever received a suspended sentence, been placed on probation, or been paroled?	No. I've never done anything against the law, so these things have never happened to me.
28.	Have you ever been in jail or prison?	No. I've never been found guilty of anything, so I've never been in jail or prison.
29.	If you answered "Yes" to any of questions 23 to 28, explain what happened.	(*Be prepared to explain why, when, and where this happened and the final result, such as no charges filed, charges dismissed, jail, probation, etc.*)
30.	Have you ever . . . a. been a habitual drunkard? b. been a prostitute, or procured anyone for prostitution? c. sold or smuggled controlled substances, illegal drugs, or narcotics? d. been married to more than one person at the same time? e. married someone in order to obtain an immigration benefit? f. helped anyone enter or try to enter the United States illegally? g. gambled illegally or received income from illegal gambling? h. failed to support your dependents or pay alimony? i. made any misrepresentation to obtain any public benefit in the United States?	a. No. I don't drink alcohol. / No. I rarely drink alcohol. b. No. I've never sold my body or paid for sex. c. No. I've never sold any illegal drugs or brought them into the country. d. No. I've never had more than one wife/husband at a time. / I've never been married to anyone. e. No. I've never married anyone to help with my immigration status. f. No. I've never helped anyone come into the country without permission. g. No. I've never gambled money in a way that's against the law. / No. I've been to a casino that's legal, but I've never gambled money in a way that's against the law. h. No. I always provide money to my _____. (children / former wife / . . .) i. No. I've never lied to receive any government assistance. I have always told the truth.
31.	Have you ever given any U.S. Government official any information or documentation that was false, fraudulent, or misleading?	No. I have never lied to an official. I have always told the truth.
32.	Have you ever lied to any U.S. government official to gain entry or admission into the United States or to gain immigration benefits while in the United States?	No. I have always told the truth.
33–36.	Have you ever been removed, excluded, or deported from the United States?*	No. I have never been ordered to leave the United States.
37.	Have you ever served in the U.S. armed forces?	Yes. I have served in the U.S. military. No. I haven't served in the U.S. military.

* Questions 33-36 are similar. They ask about removal, exclusion, or deportation proceedings against you.

38.	Are you currently a member of the U.S. armed forces?	Yes. I currently serve in the U.S. military. No. I don't currently serve in the U.S. military.
39.	Have you ever been court-martialed, administratively separated, or disciplined, or have you received an other than honorable discharge, while in the U.S. armed forces?	No. I never had a legal problem or was punished while I served in the U.S. military.
40.	Have you ever been discharged from training or service in the U.S. armed forces because you were an alien?	No. I never had to leave the U.S. military because of my immigration status.
41.	Have you ever left the United States to avoid being drafted into the U.S. armed forces?	No. I have never left the country to avoid military service.
42.	Have you ever applied for any kind of exemption from military service in the U.S. armed forces?	No. I have never asked to be excused from military service. Yes. I asked to be excused from military service because of my religion/beliefs. There is a letter from my local Selective Service board in my application file.
43.	Have you ever deserted from the U.S. armed forces?	No. I never ran away during my military service.
44.	Have you registered with the Selective Service System?	Yes. I registered for military service _____. (online / at the post office / at my high school) No. I wasn't a resident of the United States when I was between the ages of 18 and 26.
45.	Do you support the Constitution and form of government of the United States?	Yes. I believe in the Constitution as the supreme law of the land, and I believe in our form of government.
46.	Do you understand the full Oath of Allegiance to the United States?	Yes. I understand that I promise to be loyal only to the United States, that I will support the Constitution and U.S. laws, and that I will fight or work for the United States if needed.
47.	Are you willing to take the full Oath of Allegiance to the United States?	Yes. I am ready to promise to be loyal only to the United States, to support the Constitution and U.S. laws, and to fight or work for the United States if needed.
48.	If the law requires it, are you willing to bear arms on behalf of the United States?	Yes. I am willing to serve in the U.S. military and use a weapon. I am willing to serve in the U.S. military, but I cannot use a weapon because of my religion/beliefs. In my application file there's a letter that explains this. I am willing to serve the United States but not in the military because of my religion/beliefs. In my application file there's a letter that explains this.
49.	If the law requires it, are you willing to perform noncombatant services in the U.S. Armed Forces?	Yes. I am willing to serve in the U.S. military if needed. I am willing to serve the United States but not in the military because of my religion/beliefs. In my application file there's a letter that explains this.
50.	If the law requires it, are you willing to perform work of national importance under civilian direction?	Yes. I am willing to do work to help my community, my state, or the country during an emergency.

THE READING TEST

Each Reading Test item is a question. You must read one of three questions correctly. Here is the USCIS list of all words on the Reading Test.

QUESTION WORDS	CIVICS	PEOPLE	OTHER (FUNCTION)
How	American flag	Abraham Lincoln	a
What	Bill of Rights	George Washington	for
When	capital		here
Where	citizen	**PLACES**	in
Who	city	America	of
Why	Congress	United States	on
	country	U.S.	the
VERBS	Father of Our Country		to
can	government	**HOLIDAYS**	we
come	President	Presidents' Day	
do/does	right	Memorial Day	**OTHER (CONTENT)**
elects	Senators	Flag Day	colors
have/has	state/states	Independence Day	dollar bill
is/are/was/be	White House	Labor Day	first
lives/lived		Columbus Day	largest
meet		Thanksgiving	many
name			most
pay			north
vote			one
want			people
			second
			south

USCIS does not provide sample sentences for the Reading Test. Here are some possible sentences from the lessons in this textbook. For practice, make other sentences with the words in the list above.

What country is north of the United States?
What is the capital of the United States?
What city in the United States has the most people?
What are the colors on the American flag?
Who lives in the White House?
When do people in the United States vote for President?
What is one right in the Bill of Rights?
When is Thanksgiving?
Who was the first President of the United States?
Who is on the dollar bill?

_____

_____

THE WRITING TEST

Each Writing Test item is a sentence that answers a Reading Test question. You do not need to know the answer. The USCIS Officer will dictate the sentence, and you must write it correctly. You must write one of three sentences correctly to pass the Writing Test. Here is the USCIS list of all words on the Writing Test.

PEOPLE	PLACES	HOLIDAYS	OTHER (FUNCTION)	OTHER (CONTENT)
Adams	Alaska	Presidents' Day	and	blue
Lincoln	California	Memorial Day	during	dollar bill
Washington	Canada	Flag Day	for	fifty/50
	Delaware	Independence	here	first
CIVICS	Mexico	Day	in	largest
American Indians	New York City	Labor Day	of	most
capital	Washington	Columbus Day	on	north
citizens	Washington, D.C.	Thanksgiving	the	one
Civil War	United States		to	one hundred/100
Congress		**VERBS**	we	people
Father of Our	**MONTHS**	can		red
Country	February	come		second
flag	May	elect		south
free	June	have/has		taxes
freedom of speech	July	is/was/be		white
President	September	lives/lived		
right	October	meets		
Senators	November	pay		
state/states		vote		
White House		want		

USCIS does not provide sample sentences for the Writing Test. Here are some possible sentences from the lessons in this textbook. For practice, make other sentences with the words in the list above.

Canada is north of the United States.
Washington, D.C. is the capital of the United States.
New York City has the most people.
The flag is red, white, and blue.
The President of the United States lives in the White House.
People vote for President in November.
People in the United States have freedom of speech.
Thanksgiving is in November.
Washington was the first President of the United States.
President Washington is on the dollar bill.

_____

_____

100 CIVICS TEST QUESTIONS

The USCIS Officer will ask up to ten of these questions in English. You must answer six correctly to pass the Civics Test.*

* These are the official civics questions and answers provided by USCIS. For translations in Chinese, Tagalog, and Vietnamese, go to www.uscis.gov and click on "Education & Resources." Select "Civics and Citizenship Study Materials" and go to the bottom of the page for links to the translations.

AMERICAN GOVERNMENT	GOBIERNO AMERICANO
A: Principles of American Democracy	**A: Principios de la Democracia Americana**
1. What is the supreme law of the land? • the Constitution	1. ¿Cuál es la ley suprema de la nación? • la Constitución
2. What does the Constitution do? • sets up the government • defines the government • protects basic rights of Americans	2. ¿Qué hace la Constitución? • establece el gobierno • define el gobierno • protege los derechos básicos de los ciudadanos americanos
3. The idea of self-government is in the first three words of the Constitution. What are these words? • We the People	3. Las primeras tres palabras de la Constitución contienen la idea de la autodeterminación (de que el pueblo se gobierna a sí mismo). ¿Cuáles son estas palabras? • Nosotros el Pueblo
4. What is an amendment? • a change (to the Constitution) • an addition (to the Constitution)	4. ¿Qué es una enmienda? • un cambio (a la Constitución) • una adición (a la Constitución)
5. What do we call the first ten amendments to the Constitution? • the Bill of Rights	5. ¿Con qué nombre se conocen las primeras diez enmiendas a la Constitución? • la Carta de Derechos
6. What is <u>one</u> right or freedom from the First Amendment?* • speech • press • religion • petition the • assembly government	6. ¿Cuál es <u>un</u> derecho o libertad que la Primera Enmienda garantiza?* • expresión • prensa • religión • peticionar al gobierno • reunión
7. How many amendments does the Constitution have? • twenty-seven (27)	7. ¿Cuántas enmiendas tiene la Constitución? • veintisiete (27)
8. What did the Declaration of Independence do? • announced our independence (from Great Britain) • declared our independence (from Great Britain) • said that the United States is free (from Great Britain)	8. ¿Qué hizo la Declaración de Independencia? • anunció nuestra independencia (de Gran Bretaña) • declaró nuestra independencia (de Gran Bretaña) • dijo que los Estados Unidos se independizó (de Gran Bretaña)
9. What are <u>two</u> rights in the Declaration of Independence? • life • pursuit of happiness • liberty	9. ¿Cuáles son <u>dos</u> derechos en la Declaración de la Independencia? • la vida life • la búsqueda de la felicidad • la libertad

* If you are 65 years old or older and have been a legal permanent resident of the United States for 20 or more years, you may study just the 20 questions marked with an asterisk.

* Si usted tiene 65 de edad o más y hace 20 años o más que es residente permanente legal de los Estados Unidos, puede limitarse sólo al estudio de las preguntas marcadas con asterisco.

10. What is freedom of religion? • You can practice any religion, or not practice a religion.	10. ¿En qué consiste la libertad de religión? • Se puede practicar cualquier religión o no tener ninguna.
11. What is the economic system in the United States?* • capitalist economy • market economy	11. ¿Cuál es el sistema económico de los Estados Unidos?* • economía capitalista • economía del mercado
12. What is the "rule of law"? • Everyone must follow the law. • Leaders must obey the law. • Government must obey the law. • No one is above the law	12. ¿En qué consiste el "estado de derecho" (ley y orden)? • Todos deben obedecer la ley. • Los líderes deben obedecer la ley. • El gobierno debe obedecer la ley. • Nadie está por encima de la ley.
B: SYSTEM OF GOVERNMENT	**B: SISTEMA DE GOBIERNO**
13. Name one branch or part of the government.* • Congress • executive • legislative • the courts • President • judicial	13. Nombre una rama o parte del gobierno.* • Congreso • Poder ejecutivo • Poder legislativo • los tribunales • Presidente • Poder judicial
14. What stops one branch of government from becoming too powerful? • checks and balances • separation of powers	14. ¿Qué es lo que hace que una rama del gobierno no se vuelva demasiado poderosa? • pesos y contrapesos • separación de poderes
15. Who is in charge of the executive branch? • the President	15. ¿Quién está a cargo de la rama ejecutiva? • el Presidente
16. Who makes federal laws? • Congress • Senate and House (of Representatives) • (U.S. or national) legislature	16. ¿Quién crea las leyes federales? • el Congreso • el Senado y la Cámara (de Representantes) • la legislatura (nacional o de los Estados Unidos)
17. What are the two parts of the U.S. Congress?* • the Senate and House (of Representatives)	17. ¿Cuáles son las dos partes que integran el Congreso de los Estados Unidos?* • el Senado y la Cámara (de Representantes)
18. How many U.S. Senators are there? • one hundred (100)	18. ¿Cuántos senadores de los Estados Unidos hay? • cien (100)
19. We elect a U.S. Senator for how many years? • six (6)	19. ¿De cuántos años es el término de elección de un senador de los Estados Unidos? • seis (6)
20. Who is one of your state's U.S. Senators now?* • Answers will vary. [District of Columbia residents and residents of U.S. territories should answer that D.C. (or the territory where the applicant lives) has no U.S. Senators.]	20. Nombre a uno de los senadores actuales del estado donde usted vive.* • Las respuestas variarán. [Los residentes del Distrito de Columbia y los territorios de los Estados Unidos deberán contestar que el D.C. (o territorio en donde vive el solicitante) no cuenta con Senadores a nivel nacional.]
21. The House of Representatives has how many voting members? • four hundred thirty-five (435)	21. ¿Cuántos miembros votantes tiene la Cámara de Representantes? • cuatrocientos treinta y cinco (435)

22. We elect a U.S. Representative for how many years? • two (2)	22. ¿De cuántos años es el término de elección de un representante de los Estados Unidos? • dos (2)
23. Name your U.S. Representative. • Answers will vary. [Residents of territories with nonvoting Delegates or Resident Commissioners may provide the name of that Delegate or Commissioner. Also acceptable is any statement that the territory has no (voting) Representatives in Congress.]	23. Dé el nombre de su representante a nivel nacional. • Las respuestas variarán. [Los residentes de territorios con delegados no votantes o los comisionados residentes pueden decir el nombre de dicho delegado o comisionado. Una respuesta que indica que el territorio no tiene representantes votantes en el Congreso también es aceptable.]
24. Who does a U.S. Senator represent? • all people of the state	24. ¿A quiénes representa un senador de los Estados Unidos? • todas las personas del estado
25. Why do some states have more Representatives than other states? • (because of) the state's population • (because) they have more people • (because) some states have more people	25. ¿Por qué tienen algunos estados más representantes que otros? • (debido a) la población del estado • (debido a que) tienen más gente • (debido a que) algunos estados tienen más gente
26. We elect a President for how many years? • four (4)	26. ¿De cuántos años es el término de elección de un presidente? • cuatro (4)
27. In what month do we vote for President?* • November	27. ¿En qué mes votamos por un nuevo presidente?* • Noviembre
28. What is the name of the President of the United States now?* • Donald Trump • Trump	28. ¿Cómo se llama el actual Presidente de los Estados Unidos?* • Donald Trump • Trump
29. What is the name of the Vice President of the United States now? • Mike Pence • Pence	29. ¿Cómo se llama el actual Vicepresidente de los Estados Unidos? • Mike Pence • Pence
30. If the President can no longer serve, who becomes President? • the Vice President	30. Si el Presidente ya no puede cumplir sus funciones, ¿quién se vuelve Presidente? • el Vicepresidente
31. If both the President and the Vice President can no longer serve, who becomes President? • the Speaker of the House	31. Si tanto el Presidente como el Vicepresidente ya no pueden cumplir sus funciones, ¿quién se vuelve Presidente? • el Presidente de la Cámara de Representantes
32. Who is the Commander in Chief of the military? • the President	32. ¿Quién es el Comandante en Jefe de las Fuerzas Armadas? • el Presidente
33. Who signs bills to become laws? • the President	33. ¿Quién firma los proyectos de ley para convertirlos en ley? • el Presidente
34. Who vetoes bills? • the President	34. ¿Quién veta los proyectos de ley? • el Presidente
35. What does the President's Cabinet do? • advises the President	35. ¿Qué hace el Gabinete del Presidente? • asesora al Presidente

36. What are <u>two</u> Cabinet-level positions? • Secretary of Agriculture • Secretary of Commerce • Secretary of Defense • Secretary of Education • Secretary of Energy • Secretary of Health and Human Services • Secretary of Homeland Security • Secretary of Housing and Urban Development • Secretary of the Interior • Secretary of Labor • Secretary of State • Secretary of Transportation • Secretary of the Treasury • Secretary of Veterans Affairs • Attorney General • Vice President	36. ¿Cuáles son <u>dos</u> puestos a nivel de gabinete? • Secretario de Agricultura • Secretario de Comercio • Secretario de Defensa • Secretario de Educación • Secretario de Energía • Secretario de Salud y Servicios Humanos • Secretario de Seguridad Nacional • Secretario de Vivienda y Desarrollo Urbano • Secretario del Interior • Secretario del Trabajo • Secretario de Estado • Secretario de Transporte • Secretario del Tesoro • Secretario de Asuntos de Veteranos • Procurador General • Vicepresidente
37. What does the judicial branch do? • reviews laws • explains laws • resolves disputes (disagreements) • decides if a law goes against the Constitution	37. ¿Qué hace la rama judicial? • revisa las leyes • explica las leyes • resuelve disputas (desacuerdos) • decide si una ley va en contra de la Constitución
38. What is the highest court in the United States? • the Supreme Court	38. ¿Cuál es el tribunal más alto de los Estados Unidos? • la Corte Suprema de Justicia
39. How many justices are on the Supreme Court? • nine (9)	39. ¿Cuántos jueces hay en la Corte Suprema de Justicia? • nueve (9)
40. Who is the Chief Justice of the United States now? • John Roberts (John G. Roberts, Jr.)	40. ¿Quién es el Presidente actual de la la Corte Suprema de Justicia de los Estados Unidos? • John Roberts (John G. Roberts, Jr.)
41. Under our Constitution, some powers belong to the federal government. What is <u>one</u> power of the federal government? • to print money • to declare war • to create an army • to make treaties	41. De acuerdo a nuestra Constitución, algunos poderes pertenecen al gobierno federal. ¿Cuál es <u>un</u> poder del gobierno federal? • imprimir dinero • declarar la guerra • crear un ejército • suscribir tratados
42. Under our Constitution, some powers belong to the states. What is <u>one</u> power of the states? • provide schooling and education • provide protection (police) • provide safety (fire departments) • give a driver's license • approve zoning and land use	42. De acuerdo a nuestra Constitución, algunos poderes pertenecen a los estados. ¿Cuál es <u>un</u> poder de los estados? • proveer escuelas y educación • proveer protección (policía) • proveer seguridad (cuerpos de bomberos) • conceder licencias de conducir • aprobar la zonificación y uso de la tierra

43. Who is the Governor of your state now? • Answers will vary. [District of Columbia residents should answer that D.C. does not have a Governor.]	**43.** ¿Quién es el gobernador actual de su estado? • Las respuestas variarán. [Los residentes del Distrito de Columbia deben decir "no tenemos gobernador".]
44. What is the capital of your state?* • Answers will vary. [District of Columbia residents should answer that D.C. is not a state and does not have a capital. Residents of U.S. territories should name the capital of the territory.	**44.** ¿Cuál es la capital de su estado?* • Las respuestas variarán. [Los residentes del Distrito de Columbia deben contestar que el D.C. no es estado y que no tiene capital. Los residentes de los territorios de los Estados Unidos deben dar el nombre de la capital del territorio.]
45. What are the <u>two</u> major political parties in the United States?* • Democratic and Republican	**45.** ¿Cuáles son los <u>dos</u> principales partidos políticos de los Estados Unidos?* • Demócrata y Republicano
46. What is the political party of the President now? • Republican (Party)	**46.** ¿Cuál es el partido político del Presidente actual? • (Partido) Republicano
47. What is the name of the Speaker of the House of Representatives now? • (Paul) Ryan	**47.** ¿Cómo se llama el Presidente actual de la Cámara de Representantes? • (Paul) Ryan
C: Rights and Responsibilities	**C: Derechos y Responsabilidades**
48. There are four amendments to the Constitution about who can vote. Describe <u>one</u> of them. • Citizens eighteen (18) and older (can vote). • You don't have to pay (a poll tax) to vote. • Any citizen can vote. (Women and men can vote.) • A male citizen of any race (can vote).	**48.** Existen cuatro enmiendas a la Constitución sobre quién puede votar. Describa <u>una</u> de ellas. • Ciudadanos de dieciocho (18) años en adelante (pueden votar). • No se exige pagar un impuesto para votar (el impuesto para acudir a las urnas o "poll tax" en inglés). • Cualquier ciudadano puede votar. (Tanto las mujeres como los hombres pueden votar.) • Un hombre ciudadano de cualquier raza (puede votar).
49. What is one responsibility that is only for United States citizens?* • serve on a jury • vote in a federal election	**49.** ¿Cuál es una responsabilidad que corresponde sólo a los ciudadanos de los Estados Unidos?* • prestar servicio en un jurado • votar en una eleccion federal
50. Name <u>one</u> right only for United States citizens. • vote in a federal election • run for federal office	**50.** ¿Cuál es <u>un</u> derecho que pueden ejercer sólo los ciudadanos de los Estados Unidos? • votar en una eleccion federal • postularse a un cargo político federal
51. What are <u>two</u> rights of everyone living in the United States? • freedom of expression • freedom of speech • freedom of assembly • freedom to petition the government • freedom of religion • the right to bear arms	**51.** ¿Cuáles son <u>dos</u> derechos que pueden ejercer todas las personas que viven en los Estados Unidos? • libertad de expresión • libertad de la palabra • libertad de reunión • libertad para peticionar al gobierno • libertad religiosa • el derecho a portar armas

52. What do we show loyalty to when we say the Pledge of Allegiance? • the United States • the flag	52. ¿Ante qué demostramos nuestra lealtad cuando decimos el Juramento de Lealtad (Pledge of Allegiance)? • los Estados Unidos • la bandera
53. What is <u>one</u> promise you make when you become a United States citizen? • give up loyalty to other countries • defend the Constitution and laws of the United States • obey the laws of the United States • serve in the U.S. military (if needed) • serve (do important work for) the nation (if needed) • be loyal to the United States	53. ¿Cuál es <u>una</u> promesa que usted hace cuando se convierte en ciudadano de los Estados Unidos? • renunciar la lealtad a otros países • defender la Constitución y las leyes de los Estados Unidos • obedecer las leyes de los Estados Unidos • prestar servicio en las Fuerzas Armadas de los Estados Unidos (de ser necesario) • prestar servicio a (realizar trabajo importante para) la nación (de ser necesario) • ser leal a los Estados Unidos
54. How old do citizens have to be to vote for President?* • eighteen (18) and older	54. ¿Cuántos años tienen que tener los ciudadanos para votar por el Presidente?* • dieciocho (18) años en adelante
55. What are <u>two</u> ways that Americans can participate in their democracy? • vote • join a political party • help with a campaign • join a civic group • join a community group • give an elected official your opinion on an issue • call Senators and Representatives • publicly support or oppose an issue or policy • run for office • write to a newspaper	55. ¿Cuáles son <u>dos</u> maneras mediante las cuales los ciudadanos americanos pueden participar en su democracia? • votar • afiliarse a un partido político • ayudar en una campaña • unirse a un grupo cívico • unirse a un grupo comunitario • presentar su opinión sobre un asunto a un oficial elegidoe • llamar a los senadores y representantes • apoyar u oponerse públicamente a un asunto o política • postularse a un cargo político • enviar una carta o mensaje a un periódico
56. When is the last day you can send in federal income tax forms?* • April 15	56. ¿Cuál es la fecha límite para enviar la declaración federal de impuesto sobre el ingreso?* • el 15 de abril
57. When must all men register for the Selective Service? • at age eighteen (18) • between eighteen (18) and twenty-six (26)	57. ¿Cuándo deben inscribirse todos los hombres en el Servicio Selectivo? • a la edad de dieciocho (18) años • entre los dieciocho (18) y veintiséis (26) años de edad
AMERICAN HISTORY	**HISTORIA AMERICANA**
A: COLONIAL PERIOD AND INDEPENDENCE	A: ÉPOCA COLONIAL E INDEPENDENCIA
58. What is <u>one</u> reason colonists came to America? • freedom • political liberty • religious freedom • economic opportunity • practice their religion • escape persecution	58. ¿Cuál es <u>una</u> razón por la que los colonos vinieron a los Estados Unidos? • libertad • libertad política • libertad religiosa • oportunidad económica • para practicar su religión • para huir de la persecución

59. Who lived in America before the Europeans arrived? • American Indians • Native Americans	**59.** ¿Quiénes vivían en los Estados Unidos antes de la llegada de los europeos? • Indios americanos • Nativos americanos
60. What group of people was taken to America and sold as slaves? • Africans • people from Africa	**60.** ¿Qué pueblo fue traído a los Estados Unidos y vendido como esclavos? • Africanos • gente de África
61. Why did the colonists fight the British? • because of high taxes (taxation without representation) • because the British army stayed in their houses (boarding, quartering) • because they didn't have self-government	**61.** ¿Por qué lucharon los colonos contra los británicos? • debido a los impuestos altos (impuestos sin representación) • el ejército británico se quedó en sus casas (alojamiento, acuartelamiento) • no tenían autodeterminación
62. Who wrote the Declaration of Independence? • (Thomas) Jefferson	**62.** ¿Quién escribió la Declaración de Independencia? • (Thomas) Jefferson
63. When was the Declaration of Independence adopted? • July 4, 1776	**63.** ¿Cuándo fue adoptada la Declaración de Independencia? • el 4 de julio de 1776
64. There were 13 original states. Name three. • New Hampshire • Delaware • Massachusetts • Maryland • Rhode Island • Virginia • Connecticut • North Carolina • New York • South Carolina • New Jersey • Georgia • Pennsylvania	**64.** Había 13 estados originales. Nombre tres. • Nueva Hampshire • Delaware • Massachusetts • Maryland • Rhode Island • Virginia • Connecticut • Carolina del Norte • Nueva York • Carolina del Sur • Nueva Jersey • Georgia • Pennsylvania
65. What happened at the Constitutional Convention? • The Constitution was written. • The Founding Fathers wrote the Constitution.	**65.** ¿Qué ocurrió en la Convención Constitucional? • Se redactó la Constitución. • Los Padres Fundadores redactaron la Constitución
66. When was the Constitution written? • 1787	**66.** ¿Cuándo fue escrita la Constitución? • 1787
67. The Federalist Papers supported the passage of the U.S. Constitution. Name <u>one</u> of the writers. • (James) Madison • (John) Jay • (Alexander) Hamilton • Publius	**67.** Los ensayos conocidos como "Los Federalistas" respaldaron la aprobación de la Constitución de los Estados Unidos. Nombre <u>uno</u> de los autores. • (James) Madison • (John) Jay • (Alexander) Hamilton • Publius
68. What is <u>one</u> thing Benjamin Franklin is famous for? • U.S. diplomat • oldest member of the Constitutional Convention • first Postmaster General of the United States • writer of "Poor Richard's Almanac" • started the first free libraries	**68.** Mencione <u>una</u> razón por la que es famoso Benjamin Franklin. • diplomático americano • el miembro de mayor edad de la Convención Constitucional • primer Director General de Correos de los Estados Unidos • autor de "Poor Richard's Almanac" (Almanaque del Pobre Richard) • fundó las primeras bibliotecas gratuitas

69. Who is the "Father of Our Country"? • (George) Washington	**69.** ¿Quién se conoce como el "Padre de Nuestra Nación"? • (George) Washington
70. Who was the first President?* • (George) Washington	**70.** ¿Quién fue el primer Presidente?* • (George) Washington

B: 1800s	**B: Los Años 1800**
71. What territory did the United States buy from France in 1803? • the Louisiana Territory • Louisiana	**71.** ¿Qué territorio compró los Estados Unidos de Francia en 1803? • el territorio de Louisiana • Louisiana
72. Name <u>one</u> war fought by the United States in the 1800s. • War of 1812 • Mexican-American War • Civil War • Spanish-American War	**72.** Mencione <u>una</u> guerra durante los años 1800 en la que peleó los Estados Unidos. • la Guerra de 1812 • la Guerra entre México y los Estados Unidos • la Guerra Civil • la Guerra Hispanoamericana
73. Name the U.S. war between the North and the South. • the Civil War • the War between the States	**73.** Dé el nombre de la guerra entre el Norte y el Sur de los Estados Unidos. • la Guerra Civil • la Guerra entre los Estados
74. Name <u>one</u> problem that led to the Civil War. • slavery • economic reasons • states' rights	**74.** Mencione <u>un</u> problema que condujo a la Guerra Civil. • esclavitud • razones económicas • derechos de los estados
75. What was <u>one</u> important thing that Abraham Lincoln did?* • freed the slaves (Emancipation Proclamation) • saved (or preserved) the Union • led the United States during the Civil War	**75.** ¿Qué fue <u>una</u> cosa importante que hizo Abraham Lincoln?* • liberó a los esclavos (Proclamación de la Emancipación) • salvó (o preservó) la Unión • presidió los Estados Unidos durante la Guerra Civil
76. What did the Emancipation Proclamation do? • freed the slaves • freed slaves in the Confederacy • freed slaves in the Confederate states • freed slaves in most Southern states	**76.** ¿Qué hizo la Proclamación de la Emancipación? • liberó a los esclavos • liberó a los esclavos de la Confederación • liberó a los esclavos en los estados de la Confederación • liberó a los esclavos en la mayoría de los estados del Sur
77. What did Susan B. Anthony do? • fought for women's rights • fought for civil rights	**77.** ¿Qué hizo Susan B. Anthony? • luchó por los derechos de la mujer • luchó por los derechos civiles

C: RECENT AMERICAN HISTORY AND OTHER IMPORTANT HISTORICAL INFORMATION	**C: HISTORIA AMERICANA RECIENTE Y OTRA INFORMACIÓN HISTÓRICA IMPORTANTE**
78. Name <u>one</u> war fought by the United States in the 1900s.* • World War I • World War II • Korean War • Vietnam War • (Persian) Gulf War	**78.** Mencione <u>una</u> guerra durante los años 1900 en la que peleó los Estados Unidos.* • la Primera Guerra Mundial • la Segunda Guerra Mundial • la Guerra de Corea • la Guerra de Vietnam • la Guerra del Golfo (Persa)

79. Who was President during World War I? • (Woodrow) Wilson	79. ¿Quién era presidente durante la Primera Guerra Mundial? • (Woodrow) Wilson
80. Who was President during the Great Depression and World War II? • (Franklin) Roosevelt	80. ¿Quién era presidente durante la Gran Depresión y la Segunda Guerra Mundial? • (Franklin) Roosevelt
81. Who did the United States fight in World War II? • Japan, Germany, and Italy	81. ¿Contra qué países peleó los Estados Unidos en la Segunda Guerra Mundial? • Japón, Alemania e Italia
82. Before he was President, Eisenhower was a general. What war was he in? • World War II	82. Antes de ser presidente, Eisenhower era general. ¿En qué guerra participó? • Segunda Guerra Mundial
83. During the Cold War, what was the main concern of the United States? • Communism	83. Durante la Guerra Fría, ¿cuál era la principal preocupación de los Estados Unidos? • Comunismo
84. What movement tried to end racial discrimination? • civil rights (movement)	84. ¿Qué movimiento trató de poner fin a la discriminación racial? • (el movimiento en pro de los) derechos civiles
85. What did Martin Luther King, Jr. do?* • fought for civil rights • worked for equality for all Americans	85. ¿Qué hizo Martin Luther King, Jr.?* • luchó por los derechos civiles • trabajó por la igualdad de todos los ciudadanos americanos
86. What major event happened on September 11, 2001, in the United States? • Terrorists attacked the United States.	86. ¿Qué suceso de gran magnitud ocurrió el 11 de septiembre de 2001 en los Estados Unidos? • Los terroristas atacaron los Estados Unidos.
87. Name one American Indian tribe in the United States. [USCIS Officers will be supplied with a list of federally recognized American Indian tribes.] • Cherokee • Creek • Huron • Navajo • Blackfeet • Oneida • Sioux • Seminole • Lakota • Chippewa • Cheyenne • Crow • Choctaw • Arawak • Teton • Pueblo • Shawnee • Hopi • Apache • Mohegan • Inuit • Iroquois	87. Mencione una tribu de indios americanos de los Estados Unidos. [A los oficiales del USCIS se les dará una lista de tribus amerindias reconocidas a nivel federal.] • Cherokee • Creek • Huron • Navajo • Blackfeet • Oneida • Sioux • Seminole • Lakota • Chippewa • Cheyenne • Crow • Choctaw • Arawak • Teton • Pueblo • Shawnee • Hopi • Apache • Mohegan • Inuit • Iroquois

INTEGRATED CIVICS	CÍVISMO INTEGRADO
A: GEOGRAPHY	**A: GEOGRAPHY**
88. Name one of the two longest rivers in the United States. • Missouri (River) • Mississippi (River)	88. Mencione uno de los dos ríos más largos en los Estados Unidos. • (el río) Missouri • (el río) Mississippi
89. What ocean is on the West Coast of the United States? • Pacific (Ocean)	89. ¿Qué océano está en la costa oeste de los Estados Unidos? • (el océano) Pacífico
90. What ocean is on the East Coast of the United States? • Atlantic (Ocean)	90. ¿Qué océano está en la costa este de los Estados Unidos? • (el océano) Atlántico

91. Name <u>one</u> U.S. territory. • Puerto Rico • U.S. Virgin Islands • American Samoa • Northern Mariana Islands • Guam	91. Dé el nombre de <u>un</u> territorio de los Estados Unidos. • Puerto Rico • Islas Vírgenes de los Estados Unidos • Samoa Americana • Islas Marianas del Norte • Guam
92. Name <u>one</u> state that borders Canada. • Maine • Pennsylvania • Montana • New Hampshire • Ohio • Idaho • Michigan • Washington • Vermont • Minnesota • Alaska • New York • North Dakota	92. Mencione <u>un</u> estado que tiene frontera con Canadá. • Maine • Pennsylvania • Montana • Nueva Hampshire • Ohio • Idaho • Michigan • Washington • Vermont • Minnesota • Alaska • Nueva York • Dakota del Norte
93. Name <u>one</u> state that borders Mexico. • California • New Mexico • Arizona • Texas	93. Mencione <u>un</u> estado que tiene frontera con México. • California • Nuevo México • Arizona • Texas
94. What is the capital of the United States?* • Washington, D.C.	94. ¿Cuál es la capital de los Estados Unidos?* • Washington, D.C.
95. Where is the Statue of Liberty?* • New York (Harbor) • Liberty Island [Also acceptable are New Jersey, near New York City, and on the Hudson (River).]	95. ¿Dónde está la Estatua de la Libertad?* • (el puerto de) Nueva York • Liberty Island [Otras respuestas aceptables son Nueva Jersey, cerca de la Ciudad de Nueva York y (el río) Hudson.]

B: SYMBOLS	**B: SÍMBOLOS**
96. Why does the flag have 13 stripes? • because there were 13 original colonies • because the stripes represent the original colonies	96. ¿Por qué hay 13 franjas en la bandera? • porque representan las 13 colonias originales • porque las franjas representan las colonias originales
97. Why does the flag have 50 stars?* • because there is one star for each state • because each star represents a state • because there are 50 states	97. ¿Por qué hay 50 estrellas en la bandera?* • porque hay una estrella por cada estado • porque cada estrella representa un estado • porque hay 50 estados
98. What is the name of the national anthem? • The *Star-Spangled Banner*	98. ¿Cómo se llama el himno nacional? • The *Star-Spangled Banner*

C: HOLIDAYS	**C: DÍAS FERIADOS**
99. When do we celebrate Independence Day?* • July 4	99. ¿Cuándo celebramos el Día de la Independencia?* • el 4 de julio
100. Name <u>two</u> national U.S. holidays. • New Year's Day • Martin Luther King, Jr. Day • Presidents' Day • Memorial Day • Independence Day • Labor Day • Columbus Day • Veterans Day • Thanksgiving • Christmas	100. Mencione <u>dos</u> días feriados nacionales de los Estados Unidos. • el Día de Año Nuevo • el Día de Martin Luther King, Jr. • el Día de los Presidentes • el Día del Recordación • el Día de la Independencia • el Día del Trabajo • el Día de la Raza (Cristóbal Colón) • el Día de los Veteranos • el Día de Acción de Gracias • el Día de Navidad

Scripts for Listening Exercises

Unit A – Page 5

Listen and circle the correct answer.

1. A. What's your family name?
   B. Martinez.
   A. Could you spell that, please?
   B. M-A-R-T-I-N-E-Z.
2. A. What's your last name?
   B. Garza.
   A. Could you spell that, please?
   B. G-A-R-Z-A.
3. A. What's your surname?
   B. Ly.
   A. Could you spell that, please?
   B. L-Y.
4. A. What's your last name?
   B. Moreno.
   A. How do you spell that?
   B. M-O-R-E-N-O.
5. A. What's your family name?
   B. Wong.
   A. How do you spell that?
   B. W-O-N-G.
6. A. What's your surname?
   B. Mansour.
   A. Could you spell that, please?
   B. M-A-N-S-O-U-R.

Unit A – Page 9

Listen and circle the number you hear.

1. My address is thirty Main Street.
2. My address is thirteen Spring Street.
3. My address is fifty Stanley Avenue.
4. My address is forty-six fifteen Donaldson Street.
5. My address is eighteen thirty-nine Parkman Avenue.
6. My address is eight forty-two Conway Avenue.

Unit B – Page 17

Listen and circle A or B.

1. Where were you born?
2. What's your date of birth?
3. What's your place of birth?
4. When were you born?
5. Where are you from?
6. What's your birth date?

Unit 3 – Page 52

Listen and circle the correct answer.

1. Where does the President work?
2. Where does the Congress work?
3. Who makes the laws of the United States?
4. Who explains the laws of the United States?
5. Who enforces the laws of the United States?
6. Who works in the Congress of the United States?

Unit 6 – Page 100

Listen and circle the correct answer.

1. Where was the first American colony?
2. When did people from England come to the first American colony?
3. When did the Pilgrims come to America?
4. Why did the Pilgrims come to America?
5. What is the name of the colony that the Pilgrims came to?
6. What is the name of the ship that the Pilgrims sailed to America?

Unit 7 – Page 117

Listen and circle the correct answer.

1. When did the colonists sign the Declaration of Independence?
2. Where did the colonists sign the Declaration of Independence?
3. Why did the colonists sign the Declaration of Independence?
4. Who did the colonies fight during the Revolutionary War?
5. When did the colonies fight the Revolutionary War?
6. Why did the colonies fight the Revolutionary War?

Unit 10 – Page 175

Listen and circle the correct answer.

1. Who was the President during World War II?
2. Who was the President during World War I?
3. Who did the United States fight during World War II?
4. What new international organization was formed after World War II?
5. What was the main concern of the United States during the Cold War?
6. Who was a general before he was President?

Dictation Sentences for Unit Tests

Unit 1 – Page 37

1. Canada is north of the United States.
2. The capital of the United States is Washington, D.C.
3. Mexico is south of the United States.
4. Alaska is the largest state.
5. New York City has the most people.

Unit 2 – Page 45

1. The flag is red, white, and blue.
2. The United States has fifty (50) states.
3. The state of California has the most people.
4. Washington, D.C. is the capital of the United States.
5. Alaska is the largest state.

Unit 3 – Page 55

1. The Congress meets in Washington, D.C.
2. The President of the United States lives in the White House.
3. The White House is in Washington, D.C.
4. United States Senators meet in Washington, D.C.
5. The President lives in the White House in Washington, D.C.

Unit 4 – Page 75

1. Citizens of the United States can vote for the President.
2. People vote for President in November.
3. The Congress of the United States has one hundred (100) Senators.
4. Citizens in the fifty (50) states elect the Senators.
5. Citizens of the United States vote in November.

Unit 5 – Page 89

1. The people of the United States elect the President.
2. Citizens of the United States vote for the Congress.
3. We vote for the Congress in November.
4. People in the United States have freedom of speech.
5. The President lives in the White House.

Unit 6 – Page 107

1. Columbus Day is in October.
2. American Indians lived here first.
3. Thanksgiving is in November.
4. People want to be free.
5. The first Thanksgiving was in November.

Unit 7 – Page 123

1. Independence Day is in July.
2. The first President of the United States was Washington.
3. Washington, D.C. is the capital of the United States.
4. Washington was the first President of the United States.
5. People have the right to be free.

Unit 8 – Page 143

1. Washington was the Father of Our Country.
2. President Washington is on the dollar bill.
3. Washington was the first President of the United States.
4. Delaware was the first state.
5. New York City was the first capital of the United States.

Unit 9 – Page 163

1. Presidents' Day is in February.
2. Abraham Lincoln was the President during the Civil War.
3. One right people have is freedom of speech.
4. Citizens of the United States can vote for the President.
5. Alaska is the largest state in the United States.

Unit 10 – Page 183

1. Labor Day is in September.
2. People come to the United States to be free.
3. People in the United States have freedom of speech.
4. Citizens can vote for the President of the United States.
5. Citizens can vote for Senators and the President.

Unit 11 – Page 197

1. Memorial Day is in May.
2. Independence Day is in July.
3. Thanksgiving is in November.
4. Columbus Day is in October.
5. Flag Day is in June.

Unit 12 – Page 211

1. People in the United States pay taxes.
2. Citizens have the right to vote.
3. Citizens can vote for President and Congress.
4. Citizens of the United States elect the President.
5. People in the United States have to pay taxes.

Index

Adams, John, 188
Afghanistan, 178, 193–194
Alamo, the, 31
Alaska, 27, 148–149
Alaska Natives, 83
Aldrin, Buzz, 42
Allied nations, 171
Alphabet, 4
Amendments, 83–85, 87, 138–139, 141, 156–159
America, 105
American Indian tribes, 93
American Samoa, 32
America the Beautiful, 35
Anthony, Susan B., 157, 159, 161
A-number, 1, 6, 7, 10
Arizona, 27, 31, 148
Arlington, Virginia, 147, 178
Armstrong, Neil, 42
Astronauts, 42
Atlantic Ocean, 25, 27, 32, 92
Atomic bomb, 171
Austria-Hungary, 170

Bates, Katharine Lee, 35
Bill of Rights, 83, 87, 125, 138–139, 156, 159, 189
Bills, 62
Bosnia, 193
Boston Tea Party, 109–111
Branches of government, 47–63, 68–70, 82, 126, 134–137
Bush, George H.W., 173, 175, 192, 194
Bush, George W., 178, 193–194

Cabinet, 66–67, 135
California, 27, 31, 148–149
Canada, 25, 27
Capitalist economy, 78–79
Capitol, U.S., 47, 50, 134
Caribbean Sea, 32
Carter, James Earl, 192, 194
Checks and balances, 48
Chief Justice, 57, 68–70
China, 191
Christmas, 186
Civic participation, 12, 24, 38, 46, 56, 72, 76, 90, 108, 124, 144, 164, 198, 204–205, 212
Civics test dialogs, USCIS, 34, 43, 53, 71, 87, 104, 121, 141, 161, 181, 208

Civil rights movement, 165, 176–177, 179
Civil War, 145, 149–155, 189
Clinton, William J., 193–194
Cold War, 172
Colonies, 40, 96–100, 102–103, 110–118, 126–129
Colorado, 35, 148
Columbus, Christopher, 91, 92
Columbus Day, 92, 186–187
Commander-in-Chief, 62, 135
Communism, 172, 175
Confederacy, 150–151, 153–154, 195
Congress, 47–53, 58–61, 134
Connecticut, 128–129
Constitution, 68, 82–87, 125–127, 131, 138–139, 156–157, 159
Constitutional Convention, 126–127, 131–133, 140, 188
Cuba, 148

Dates, 13–15, 18–19, 21
Declaration of Independence, 109, 114–118, 121, 188
Delaware, 128–129
Democratic form of government, 78
Democratic Party, 194–195, 200–201
Depression, 165, 170, 190

Economic system, 78–79
Eisenhower, Dwight D., 171, 175, 190, 195
Elections, 200–203
Emancipation Proclamation, 152–154, 189, 195
England, 96
English test, USCIS, 214–225
Executive branch, 47–49, 57, 62–67, 70, 135
Expansion, 148–149

Family members, 14–15
Federalist Papers, 130–131, 141, 189, 195
First Amendment, 83–85, 87, 138–139, 156, 161
Flag, U.S., 39–46
Flag Day, 187
Florida, 102, 148–149
Ford, Gerald, 191

Form N-400, 5, 7, 11, 15, 22, 216–225
Founding Fathers, 126–127, 132–133, 188–189
Fourth of July, 119, 186–187
France, 132–133, 148, 170
Franklin, Benjamin, 132–133, 141

Gateway Arch, 31
Geography, 25–38
Georgia, 128–129
Germany, 170–171
Gettysburg Address, 145, 155
Golden Gate Bridge, 31
Governor, 77, 80–81
Grand Canyon National Park, 31
Great Britain, 110–115, 121, 146, 148–149
Great Depression, 165, 170, 190
Great Society programs, 191
Guam, 32, 148

Hamilton, Alexander, 130–131, 141, 195
Hawaii, 148–149, 171
Henry, Patrick, 110
Holidays, 91, 102, 119, 152, 167, 176, 185–187
Hollywood, 31
Hollywood sign, 31
House of Representatives, 57, 60–61, 71, 134
Hudson River, 30
Hussein, Saddam, 193
Hutchinson, Anne, 97–100

"I Have a Dream" speech, 177
Idaho, 27
Illinois, 194
Immigrants, 165, 168
Impeachment, 193
Income taxes, 157
Independence Day, 119, 185–187
Independence Hall, 114–115, 118
Indians, American, 92–93
Industrial Revolution, 166
Internet activities, 38, 46, 56, 76, 90, 108, 124, 164, 184, 198
Interview dialogs, USCIS, 4, 10, 16, 18, 20, 21, 213–225
Inventions, 132, 165–166

Iraq, 173, 193–194
Italy, 171
Iwo Jima, 42

Jamestown, 96, 98–100, 105
Jamestown Settlement, 105
Japan, 171
Jay, John, 130–131, 141, 195
Jefferson, Thomas, 109, 114–115, 118, 121, 188, 195
Johnson, Lyndon B., 191
Judicial branch, 47–53, 68–70, 136

Kennedy, John F., 190
Key, Francis Scott, 146–147
King, Rev. Martin Luther, Jr., 176–177, 179
Korean War, 172–173
Kosovo, 193
Kuwait, 173

Labor Day, 167, 185–187
Labor movement, 165, 167
Labor unions, 167
Landmarks, famous U.S., 30–31
Legislative branch, 47–53, 57–61, 70, 134
Liberty Bell, 30
Lincoln, Abraham, 145, 152–155, 189, 195
Louisiana Territory, 148–149, 188, 195

Madison, James, 130–131, 141, 189, 195
Maine, 27
Map, U.S., 25, 26
Map activities, 28, 95
March on Washington, 176
Marines, 42
Market economy, 78–79
Martin Luther King, Jr. Day, 176, 185–187
Maryland, 128–129
Massachusetts, 96–97, 105, 110, 128–129
Massachusetts Bay Colony, 97–99
Mayflower, 91, 96, 100
Memorial Day, 185–187
Mexican-American War, 148–149
Mexico, 25, 27
Michigan, 27
Minnesota, 27